Anti-Immigrantism in Western Democracies

This book critically examines the various practices of anti-immigrantism in three Western democracies, the United States, the United Kingdom, and France, within the context of globalization and questions our understanding of the state.

Anti-Immigrantism in Western Democracies draws upon the works of Gilles Deleuze and Felix Guattari, and analyzes their understanding of desire, its forms and its relation to the social order. Doty uses these concepts as a way to comprehend the forces at work in the social, political, and economic life, to explore the impulses which move society toward various practices and policies, and finally to understand statecraft.

In this innovative work the author concludes that immigration is an exemplary site of the manifestation of the desire for order and security in a world where things are perceived to be under threat and investigates the concept of neo-racism and its relationship to immigration policies. It will interest students and researchers of International Relations, Migration Studies, and Cultural Studies.

Roxanne Lynn Doty is an associate professor in the Department of Political Science at Arizona State University. Her research interests include race and international relations, immigration, and international relations theory.

The Routledge/RIPE series in global political economy

Series Editors: Otto Holman, Marianne Marchand (*Research Centre for International Political Economy, University of Amsterdam*) Henk Overbeek (*Free University, Amsterdam*) and Marianne Franklin (*University of Amsterdam*)

This series, published in association with the *Review of International Political Economy*, provides a forum for current debates in international political economy. The series aims to cover all the central topics in IPE and to present innovative analyzes of emerging topics. The titles in the series seek to transcend a state-centred discourse and focus on three broad themes:

* the nature of the forces driving globalisation forward
* resistance to globalisation
* the transformation of the world order.

The series comprises two strands:

The *RIPE series in global political economy* aims to address the needs of students and teachers, and the titles will be published in hardback and paperback. Titles include:

Transnational Classes and International Relations
Kees van der Pijl

Gender and Global Restructuring
Sightings, sites and resistances
Edited by Marianne H. Marchand and Anne Sisson Runyan

Global Political Economy
Contemporary theories
Edited by Ronen Palan

Ideologies of Globalization
Contending visions of a New World Order
Mark Rupert

The Clash within Civilisations
Coming to terms with cultural conflicts
Dieter Senghaas

Global Unions?
Theory and strategies of organized labour in the global
political economy
Edited by Jeffrey Harrod and Robert O'Brien

Political Economy of a Plural World
Critical reflections on power, morals and civilizations
Robert Cox with Michael Schechter

The Routledge/RIPE studies in global political economy is a forum
for innovative new research intended for a high-level specialist read-
ership, and the titles will be available in hardback only. Titles include:

1 **Globalization and Governance***
   Edited by Aseem Prakash and Jeffrey A. Hart

2 **Nation-States and Money**
   The past, present and future of national currencies
   Edited by Emily Gilbert and Eric Helleiner

3 **The Global Political Economy of Intellectual Property Rights**
   The new enclosures?
   Christopher May

4 **Integrating Central Europe**
   EU expansion and Poland, Hungary and the Czech Republic
   Otto Holman

5 **Capitalist Restructuring, Globalisation and the Third Way**
   Lessons from the Swedish model
   J. Magnus Ryner

6 **Transnational Capitalism and the Struggle**
   over European Integration
   Bastiaan van Apeldoorn

* Also available in paperback.

7 World Financial Orders
An historical international political economy
Paul Langley

8 The Changing Politics of Finance in Korea and Thailand
From deregulation to debacle
Xiaoke Zhang

9 Anti-Immigrantism in Western Democracies
Statecraft, desire, and the politics of exclusion
Roxanne Lynn Doty

10 The Political Economy of European Unemployment
Edited by Henk Overbeek

11 Rethinking International Political Economy
*Edited by Mary Ann Tétreault, Robert A. Denemark,
Kurt Burch and Kenneth P. Thomas*

12 Rediscovering International Relations Theory
Matthew Davies and Michael Niemann

Anti-Immigrantism in Western Democracies
Statecraft, desire, and the politics of exclusion

Roxanne Lynn Doty

Routledge
Taylor & Francis Group

LONDON AND NEW YORK

First published 2003
by Routledge
2 Park Square, Milton Park, Abingdon, Oxon, OX14 4RN

Simultaneously published in the USA and Canada
by Routledge
270 Madison Ave, New York NY 10016

Routledge is an imprint of the Taylor & Francis Group

Transferred to Digital Printing 2006

Typeset in Sabon by
Newgen Imaging Systems (P) Ltd, Chennai, India

British Library Cataloguing in Publication Data
A catalogue record for this book is available from the British Library

Library of Congress Cataloging in Publication Data
Doty, Roxanne Lynn.
    Anti-immigrantism in western democracies: statecraft, desire, and
the politics of exclusion/Roxanne Lynn Doty.
        p. cm.
    Includes bibliographical references and index.
    1. United States – Emigration and immigration – Government policy.
    2. Great Britain – Emigration and immigration – Government policy.
    3. France – Emigration and immigration – Government policy.
    4. Racism – Political aspects – United States. 5. Racism – Political
aspects – Great Britain. 6. Racism – Political aspects – France. I. Title.
    JV6483 .D68 2003
    325'.1–dc21   2002151226

ISBN10: 0–415–29979–9 (hbk)
ISBN10: 0–415–40668–4 (pbk)

ISBN13: 978–0–415–29979–4 (hbk)
ISBN13: 978–0–415–40668–0 (pbk)

Contents

Acknowledgments		viii
Series editor's preface		ix
1	Statecraft's desire and anti-immigrantism in Western democracies	1
2	Dangers and differences in a globalizing world	18
3	Mark your territory	32
4	The empire comes home to Britain	44
5	*Seuil de tolerance*	58
6	In closing and reflection	73
	Notes	77
	Bibliography	99
	Index	111

Acknowledgments

Research for this study was supported by a grant from the Harry Frank Guggenheim Foundation. I would like to thank Cynthia Weber and an anonymous reviewer for their helpful comments and suggestions. This book is dedicated to the human beings who travel to the edges; the deserts, the seas, the tunnels of the world that have become death traps to those who must, for various reasons, cross the artificial borders constructed by the power, desire, and insecurity that lurks in the many elusive centers of our contemporary world. In memory and respect, especially, for all of those who have died in the process. All royalties from the sale of this book are being donated to the Florence Immigrant and Refugee Rights Project, Inc. in Florence, Arizona.

The authors and publishers would like to thank the following for granting permission to reproduce material in this work:

Cambridge University Press for sections that appear in Chapter 4, originally printed in *Review of International Studies*, 22(3) (1996). *Millennium: Journal of International Studies* for Chapter 5, originally printed in *Millennium*, 28(3) (1999).

Series editor's preface

Despite a number of widely publicized instances of anti-immigrant sentiment, government policies, and party political platforms in Western Europe, and the United States of late, this is not a new phenomenon. What is new, and more striking since the events of September 11, 2001, is the vehemence of concern being expressed about the perceived negative social and economic impacts of populations from poorer economies moving, for the most part, to richer ones. It is the intensity of this fear and loathing, the security measures, border controls, and rhetoric that goes with it, that is at the heart of this latest book in the RIPE Series in Global Political Economy by Roxanne Doty.

In her own words, Doty sets out to do three things; reconceptualize "the state" as "practices of statecraft," put forward the notion of "desire as the non-essentializable essence of statecraft," and, third, "suggest that racism is significantly implicated in contemporary practices of statecraft, that it is an expression of the desire for order." By implication, the practices of past and present international relations are also taken to task here. At a time when xenophobia has a new target – the Islamic fundamentalist/terrorist – Doty's book is a timely intervention in a sensitive debate. Doty takes a clear and provocative position towards contemporary patterns of immigration and how these relate, uneasily, to processes of globalization by arguing that anti-immigrant attitudes have always been part of Western democratic practices of "statecraft." But she goes further to argue that these practices indicate a strong undercurrent of "desire" – for order; that desire in this sense is both repressive and potentially liberating. Large-scale population movements and responses to them along with the borderless characteristics of globalization simply underscore this tension. Doty illustrates her point by way of the immigration policies of France, England, and the United States in recent years. Her goal is to

show where "desire lurks; within anxieties about order, divisions
between the inside and the outside, insecurities over who belongs and
who does not." In the midst of public and scholarly debates raging in
Western democracies about the desirability (*sic*) and efficacy of granting asylum and then eventually residence permits to refugees and
other immigrants, the concept of desire is a radically novel way to
think about these complex forces.

Doty draws on the work of Deleuze and Guattari, who apply a
psychodynamic conceptualization of capitalism – and by association
the Westphalian state – as a "desiring machine." State apparatuses,
policy-making, and legislation can be seen as different ways of
"channelling, organizing, inscribing" desire. Doty takes this to meet
the specific control mechanisms being brought to bear on the contemporary "problems" of immigration, and especially that coming
from the so-called Third World. These mechanisms include border
controls at the Mexican–Californian and French–British points of
entry for all travellers; violent forms of detention and deportation for
those who have exhausted their legal possibilities or have been designated as unsuitable candidates for citizenship in all three countries,
openly racist attacks on individuals of Moroccan and Turkish origin
in Germany and Spain. In Doty's study, desire can be seen to be
working in the tension between the centrifugal and centripetal tendencies of modern statecraft; between the drive to control the popu-
lace from the centre and the individualistic liberal ideals that underpin
democratic theory and institution building in the West. In this respect,
the desiring machine of modern democratic statecraft (the making
and practices of nation-states and their co-requisite axes of identity
formation) is inherently schizophrenic and paranoid at the same time.
Doty shows, lucidly and powerfully, how these two tendencies are
all too apparent in contemporary anti-immigrantism and the "new
racism" that this underscores.

The *RIPE Series in GPE* is pleased to publish this important theoretical and empirical contribution to the debates around identity-
formation, culture and society, and the socio-cultural implications of
unabated – and unarticulated – globalization. In the spirit of some
other RIPE Series authors (Rupert, Senghaas, Cox), Roxanne Doty's
study of a new politics of exclusion that focuses on a racialized and
victimized Other in three Western democracies does not pull any
punches. Her examination of overt and covert anti-immigrant
practices – in the media, prisons, passport control points of airports
and harbours of the Unites States, France, and Great Britain – is a
provocative and succinct examination of how three self-consciously

"free" and "open" societies work towards the "never fully realized desire for order" in different ways. Without resorting to easy polemics or glib statistics, Doty traces the everydayness of the new racism from an unsettling angle. It is not the result of individual's racist behavior but is at the heart of modern statecraft itself as democracies try to achieve the impossible – physically seal off the nation-state from that which lies outside – the other, the undesirable.

Marianne Franklin
Otto Holman
Marianne Marchand
Henk Overbeek
Amsterdam, November 2002

1 Statecraft's desire and anti-immigrantism in Western democracies

Beginnings

> Facing north, the priest said, Desire is lack (how could it not lack what it desires?).... Then facing south, the priest linked desire to pleasure. For there are hedonistic, even orgiastic, priests. Desire will be assuaged by pleasure; and not only will the pleasure obtained silence desire for a moment but the process of obtaining it is already a way of interrupting it, of instantly discharging it and unburdening oneself of it. Pleasure as discharge; the priest carries out the second sacrifice, named masturbation. Then, facing east, he exclaimed: Jouissance is impossible, but impossible jouissance is inscribed in desire. For that, in its very impossibility, is the Ideal, the "manque-a-jouir that is life." The priest carried out the third sacrifice, phantasy or the thousand and one nights, the one hundred twenty days, while the men of the East chanted: Yes, we will be your phantasy, your ideal and impossibility, yours and also our own. The priest did not turn west. But that is where desire was lurking.[1]

Let us turn West then and begin with desire defined not as lack or phantasy or pleasure but, as a force that haunts modern societies producing constructions of order, identity, and determinacy. For it is in the West that the project of creating order and taming chaos in its many forms has ostensibly been the most successful and where the priests who both revel in this achievement and express anxiety over threats to it are the most vocal. Let us also begin with one particular global phenomenon that has resulted in a multitude of highly dispersed and varied battles to reconstruct order; human beings moving across sovereign territorial space and the practices these movements have given rise to. Of course, we could begin elsewhere, in another place, with another issue. There are many issues today in many parts of the world that are understood to threaten order and security, that evoke desires for a center that holds, a foundation that does not fall apart, a rationality beyond desire. Terrorism, the international drug trade, the global transmission of infectious diseases would name just a few of these issues.[2] While we could begin with any one of these, immigration seems a particularly appropriate place to begin evoking as it does such intensities of feeling, such concerns over identity and belonging, eliciting widespread interest from high-level government officials to academics, to the popular press, and the general public. So, let us begin with this locus of desire, this "new global reality" created by post Second World War migrations of people from poor countries of the "Third World" to rich industrialized countries of the West, which has coincided with and been an integral part of the much discussed and variously defined phenomenon called globalization.[3] Human migration has given rise to some of the same fears expressed regarding the unfettered movement of goods, services, and capital across global space. These concerns revolve around the issue of sovereignty and the continued viability of "the state" and the community it ostensibly represents in the face of unprecedented openness and fluidity that characterizes much of contemporary global life. People, however, are very different from money, bananas, cigarettes, and automobiles, and the consequences of their movements have more profound effects on societies.

But why begin with desire? Clearly there are many concepts I could begin with. Many have written and spoken about immigration, never uttering, never even whispering the word desire. Much has been written about the tension between the erosion of territorial boundaries precipitated by globalization on the one hand and the need to reassert sovereign control over borders on the other hand without evoking the elusive and slippery concept of desire. Much has been written about that amorphous entity that must always be summoned when we discuss boundaries and sovereign authority, "the state" without ever linking it to desire. But, of course, this is precisely why I begin with desire – because while we have so many words with which to talk about immigration, sovereign boundaries, and "the state," desire has not been one of them. This is unfortunate because I think it underlies so many practices that aim to create order, to banish ambiguity, to create stability and fixedness, statecraft being exemplary among these practices. This silence, this unconscious censuring of desire, takes on the importance of a scream that echoes throughout the many diverse sites where statecraft does its work; from the journals of academia to the offices of government leaders to the streets of major cities and small rural villages to the many border crossing areas in our globalized world.

Gilles Deleuze and Felix Guattari, whose ideas I draw upon say "There is only desire and the social, and nothing else."[4] An exaggeration you may say, but perhaps not. It is at least an interesting proposition to ponder and surely no more absurd that the often criticized, but still widely tolerated and even revered assumption that "the state" is a unitary, rational actor, or the obsessive though arguably banal debates over whether this unitary, rational actor pursues absolute or relative gains.[5] So, beginning with the movement of human beings and the concept of desire, I explore an understanding of "the state" that suggests there is no such thing as "the state" and that places desire at the core of this non-thing. I take seriously Deleuze and Guattari's, invitation to "lift a dynamism" out of their work and "incorporate it in a foreign medium, whether painting or politics."[6]

Immigration in the age of globalization

The movement of human beings across geographic space is certainly not a new phenomenon nor is their movement across territorially sovereign states of the Western industrialized world. Even after the development of the nation-state and the idea of legally tying populations to territorial units in the sixteenth and seventeenth centuries, people continued to migrate in large numbers. Two things *are* however, different about post Second World War migrations; the places these human beings come from and the fact that their movement takes place at a time when there is so much other movement in the world, so many things in flux, so many flows across so much space that space itself is often defined by speed and movement. While proportionally small, the number of people migrating from the "Third World" to Western industrialized countries is significant. Until the 1960s, 80 percent of immigrants to the United States, Canada, and Australia came from other industrialized countries. By the end of the 1980s, 82 percent came from developing countries. The top source countries for US immigration in 1998 were Mexico (19.9 percent), mainland China (5.6 percent), India (5.5 percent), the Philippines (5.2 percent), and the Dominican Republic (3.1 percent), reflecting a shift toward Latin American and Asian immigration since the 1960s.[7] Similarly, in most European OECD countries the proportion of foreign residents from other EU countries has contracted significantly. Three North African countries accounted for a fairly steady 43 percent of the migration flow into France in the mid-1980s. Southern European countries, which have traditionally supplied workers in large numbers to northern Europe are increasingly becoming hosts to growing numbers of migrants from northern Africa and eastern Europe.[8] By the late 1990s, there were officially 11 million non-EU citizens living in the fifteen member European Union, including 5 million in Germany, 2.2 million in France, and 1 million in the United Kingdom.[9] Another source puts this total figure at 13 million.[10]

Statistics though, are not as important as the reactions these immigrants have elicited and the perceived consequences of their movement. That the presence of a significant number of "Third World" immigrants is often perceived as threatening was exemplified by Margaret Thatcher's oft quoted (1978) remark that "People are really rather afraid that this country might be swamped by people with a different culture."[11] Though Thatcher expressed this concern rather blatantly, it can also be found in numerous other utterings by numerous other government officials as well as academics. This generally takes the form of a concern with the number of foreigners a society can absorb without experiencing conflict and a disruption to powerful though ambiguous things like identity, national security, and unity. Myron Weiner suggests that advanced industrialized democracies risk being destabilized by massive influxes of unwanted immigrants, refugees, and asylum-seekers.[12] Samuel Huntington argues that the failure to control borders is the single biggest threat to national security in the United States.[13] Arthur Schlesinger Jr refers to the "historic idea of a unifying American identity" as being in peril.[14] As the advance of the European Union encroaches on the national sovereignty of its member countries, these countries once haunted by the specter of communism are now haunted by "the outsider" and ultra right political parties garner support by playing upon fears of threats to national identities caused by immigration.[15] These concerns, so widely disseminated across Western landscapes, are clearly not referring to immigrants from other Western countries. In fact, in many instances the term "immigrant" has come to refer only to people from the "Third World" and the "immigration problem" is associated almost exclusively with people from "Third World" countries moving to Western industrialized countries.[16] The issue of "race" inevitably raises its head and concerns over capacities to absorb and "thresholds of tolerance" are often thinly veiled codes for a contemporary form of racism. Peter Brimlow's *Alien Nation* is the most blatant in this regard.[17]

The other significant feature of contemporary migrations is that they occur within the context of globalization, itself an extremely complex, rather amorphous, and multi-faceted phenomenon, which also has resulted in many anxieties, most notably concerning "the state" and its sovereignty, autonomy, and ability to control what crosses its borders. Much of the recent academic literature on global-ization focuses on "the state" and the issue of order and disorder.[18] What has become known as the "globalization thesis" suggests that states have been weakened in the sense that they are often unable to fully control the movement of goods, capital, people, and culture, which are all elements of globalization. Losing control over borders erodes the effectiveness of states, undermines their sovereignty, and by extension raises questions about the type of international system that may be emerging. For example, Rosenau understands globalization as "a wholly new set of processes, a separate form of world politics."[19] Regarding immigration this suggests that forces much more powerful than states are at work making governments relatively ineffective in controlling what crosses their borders. Sovereign state borders are seen as largely irrelevant in the face of economic and other incentives that present an overwhelming attraction to those seeking to cross both legally and illegally. This view is fairly widespread among students of immigration and has been amply articulated. Paul Kennedy argued that great waves of migration will continue into the twenty-first cen-tury and that enhanced efforts of states to control their borders are unlikely to succeed. Hamilton and Holder suggested that international migration posed new challenges to state sovereignty.[20] In a similar vein, others argue that the value of national citizenship is being dimin-ished in that migrants can claim rights once reserved exclusively for citizens.[21] While this view is not new, it continues to frame the immigration issue for many.

Of course, not everyone agrees that globalization leads to the increasing irrelevance of territorial borders or diminishes the power of "the state." For some, globalization depends upon political frame-works and "the state" is essential to this.[22] Some scholars argue that the state is still very much alive and well even if it often acts in a some-what contradictory and schizophrenic manner. Andreas suggests that the "wall around the west" is by design highly permeable and that any erosion of national borders is a matter of choice.[23] And certainly, the idea that the value of citizenship is declining is quite debatable. Just ask Jimmy Johnson, the Liberian refugee who has been in a US prison for six years or the thousands of other undocumented asylum-seekers who have been held in US prisons since arrival without bail and virtually without rights.[24]

Which position is correct? As with most academic debates in inter-national relations, neither of the conflicting views is necessarily wrong. Some official government practices promote various aspects of globalization while at the same time there are forces at work, which are beyond the effective control of governments. As Peter Andreas notes, the loss-of-control theme can serve as a powerful narrative that obscures the ways in which government practices themselves can create the very conditions that generate calls for and justify increased state authority.[25] The debate takes on significance only within a context where one is seeking some foundational understanding of what "the state" is, which of course presupposes that "the state" is in fact some thing or entity whose essence can be clearly defined and demarcated. Underlying concerns about sovereignty and the ability of states to control their borders is the presumption of a clearly defined interior separated from an exterior. The understanding of "the state" offered in this study departs from this presumption.

What is important for this study is that the two features of contemporary immigration, the sources of the immigrants and the context of globalization, articulate with one another resulting in anxieties that coalesce around the issue of order. "Third World" immigrants bring with them preconceptions and stereotypes involving cultural and other differences that are often deemed threatening to a cohesive national identity that is foundational to this interior. Questions of who belongs and who does not, what is considered domestic and what is considered international, what is on the inside and what is on the outside are profoundly disturbing to the dichotomies the academic discipline of international relations holds dear to its rational heart. That immigrants are coming from Third World countries, in one sense, raises concerns about order on the inside. But within the context of globalization the very notion of an inside is problematic. What is it that distinguishes this relatively tranquil realm of order and belonging, where one moves through life with a measure (or at least the illusion) of predictability, where one feels a degree of security in the ground beneath one's feet, where one knows just who one is and most certainly who one is not from that other realm of anarchy and ambiguity where nothing is certain least of all the precise point at which these two realms can be differentiated? This non-place that immigration so insistently points us toward is precisely where desire lurks; within anxieties about order, divisions between the inside and the outside, insecurities over who belongs and who does not. This is where desire does its productive work. This is where we must look for "the state."

The ambivalence of order

How to bring the concept of desire, so difficult to elucidate and theorize into international relations – a discipline so suffocated with reifications, essentializations, so obsessed with definitional precision? I will not even pretend to any aspiration to make desire a scientific concept. [26] Nor is there any truly compelling reason to think that subjecting desire to the rigors and certitudes of science would necessarily be particularly enlightening. Let us not operationalize the life out of it, strip it down to a sterile, inert construct. In all its multiplicities, fuzziness, and slipperiness desire still offers us a way to think about the forces at work in the social, political, economic, and even academic realms, a way to conceptualize the coming together and crystallizing of diverse energies and impulses in societies that move them in certain directions, toward various practices and policies. Specifically for this study, desire gives us a new way to think about statecraft, that all pervasive practice that is arguably as amorphous and multiple as desire itself. As a way of getting at how desire is important for understanding statecraft, let me begin by briefly discussing some tensions that are present in social, political, and economic life and that are especially prevalent today and particularly relevant to understanding the relationships between globalization, "the state," and immigration.

Bauman suggests that the task of order or "order as a task" is arguably the least possible among the impossible tasks that modernity sets for itself, but also the least disposable among the indispensable.[27] The tension between the essentially necessary task of creating order and the ultimate impossibility of doing so is manifested in a variety of tensions that characterize the modern nation-state and the economic, social, and political processes that traverse it. Two important thinkers have called attention to this tension in interesting ways. Karl Polanyi's work called our attention to one aspect of this tension manifested in the double movement of society, that is, the principle of economic liberalism and the principle of social protection.[28] Polanyi suggested that the self-adjusting market of capitalism could not exist for any length of time without annihilating society. No society could stand the effects of "the commodity fiction," that is, the principle that the market mechanism should be the sole determinant for human social, economic, and political relations. Yet the fiction that land, labor, and money are commodities must be upheld because there is no other way of organizing production for the market in a capitalist society.[29]

A similar kind of tension animates the writings of Foucault and others on "governmentality" in the notion that "society" makes itself out of the tension between the centrifugal forces of economic egoisms and the centripetal forces of noneconomic interests whereby individuals espouse the well-being of the family, the clan, the nation. Foucault locates what is specific and original in the liberal treatment of population in the discovery of economic man as a subject of interests, individual preferences, and choices, which are irreducible (cannot be explained from any other, more fundamental causal principle) and nontransferable (no external agency can supplant or constrain the individual determination of preferences). The subject of interest perpetually outflanks the scope of self-imposed limitation that constitutes the subject of law. Quoting Foucault, Colin Gordon suggests that

> Liberalism's real moment of beginning is, for Foucault, the moment of formulation of "this incompatibility between the non-totalizable multiplicity which characterizes subjects of interest and the totalizing unity of the juridical sovereign." This means that liberalism's main task must be that of devising a new definition of the governmental domain which can avert the hazardous alternatives (equally prejudicial of the integrity of governmental reason) of either excising the market from the field of sovereignty, or downgrading the economic sovereign into a mere functionary of political economy.... What liberalism undertakes ... is the construction of a complex domain of governmentality, within which economic and juridical sovereignty can alike be situated as relative moments, partial aspects of a more englobing element. The key role which it comes to play in this effort of construction and invention is, for Foucault, the characteristic trait of the liberal theory of civil society.[30]

Foucault and Polanyi convey to us a sense of perpetual movement and flow on the one hand and forces at work to temper or halt these movements on the other hand. For Polanyi, movement is expressed in terms of the "self-adjusting" market that runs roughshod over everything in its path decoding land, labor, and money, turning them into deterritorialized commodities and threatening to destroy the social order upon which the market ultimately depends. Social protection measures provide a countervailing force that alleviates to some degree the negative impact of the market and ironically perhaps creates the conditions by which the "commodity fiction" itself can be reproduced. For Foucault, the non-totalizable multiplicity of economic interests are in a condition of constant tension with the subject of law, the subject of self-imposed limitation, which is part of the totalizing unity of the juridical sovereign. The feat of government (broadly defined to include "civil society") then is to manage these tensions, to construct the complex domain of governmentality. This domain is never fixed, never fully stable, always in the process of being produced and reproduced. The possibility of failure always looms. In our current era of globalization these tensions are seemingly more visible and less manageable than previously, though perhaps not. Tensions have certainly always existed. Maybe we are just more aware of them today. Maybe they are just more widely discussed today because of globalization or because of the proliferation of academic writings due to imperatives to publish, or because of the media or the Internet. I certainly do not wish to suggest a golden, tension-free time of stability and fixed domains. Regardless, the distinction between what is inside the domestic and what is outside of its scope has always been essential to managing these tensions and fixing, however provisionally, the domestic in opposition to the international. Social protection measures and domains of governmentality have been fixed within the domestic realm. Domestic social protection measures such as minimum wage, health benefits, and so on have extended the realm of governmentality and, while tempering the affects of the "self-adjusting" market, have also enabled the coding of the labor of human beings as a commodity to be bought and sold thus reproducing the very situations that create the need for social protection in the first place. Social protection measures, among other things, have also functioned to effect the dividing line between domestic and international. Globalization disrupts this, breaks the neat lines that distinguish the inside from the outside, creates new lines, new connections.

While desire does not enter into Foucault's and Polanyi's discussion in any explicit way, the tensions that are key to their works illustrate the two poles of desire (the paranoiac pole and the schizophrenic pole) found in Deleuze and Guattari's social theory of desire and, which I argue are central to statecraft, particularly in this era of globalization. Liberal states and self-protection measures are embedded within societies that are always in the process of being decoded, deterritorialized, but whose very identity depends upon continual processes of recoding and reterritorialization. Societies are constituted out of both the forces that perpetually defy and move away from any fixed center (what Deleuze and Guattari would call schizophrenic forces) and by forces that continually construct the effect of a fixed center of being (forces Deleuze would call paranoiac) whereby the identity, welfare, and unity of bounded groups are promoted.[31] Desire is at the core of both of these processes and underlies the various productions of the inside realms of social protection, governmentality and order as distinguished from the outside realm of anarchy and disorder. This, I suggest, is statecraft at its most fundamental. *Statecraft is desire.*

Desire and "the state"

The truth of the matter is that social production is purely and simply desiring production itself under determinate conditions. We maintain that the social field is immediately invested by desire, that it is the historically determined product of desire.[32]

Desire is an unbounded, free-floating energy, which becomes coded and channeled in particular ways as it attaches itself to the social body whose prime function is to codify its flows, inscribe them, channel and regulate them. Society is a social space where the essential thing is to mark and be marked.[33] Desire is not internal to pregiven, individual subjects, nor is it understood in terms of an object the individual subject lacks or some transcendent ideal of phantasy. Deleuze and Guattari give analytic priority to the social and the forces and flows that traverse it. Forces give rise to thought, to action. They act upon other forces giving them senses and values. Forces synthesize and connect with other forces, affirming one another. Desire is constituted by the connection and affirmation of forces. Connolly's reference to desire as an organization of diffuse corporeal energies into specific pathways, which are never exhausted by any particular pattern and thus resist totalistic theorizing is consistent with Deleuze and Guattari's conception of desire.[34] The channeling, organizing, inscribing of desire is accomplished through a wide array of practices, which enable communication, create meanings, values, hierarchies, inclusions, and exclusions.

Every society organizes, codes, and represses desire in particular ways thereby creating networks of desire. Desire invests all of a social field, its most repressive as well as its potentially liberating impulses, the status quo, as well as the revolutionary. So, while desire is on the one hand free-floating, explosive, capable of calling into question and destroying the established order, it is also always produced under determinate conditions and organized into specific networks wherein it can be repressive. Deleuze and Guattari locate the tension between openness and closure, fluidity and fixedness in two poles of desire; the schizophrenic and the paranoiac poles. The schizophrenic pole deterritorializes and threatens to destroy the codes that inscribe meaning to social forms. The paranoiac pole presses for order and contains an inherent tendency toward despotism, repression, fascism. Modern societies oscillate between these two poles balancing them in a variety of ways. It is not, however, a matter of thinking in terms of two opposed and mutually exclusive expressions of desire. Rather, it is a dynamic and simultaneous process akin to Derrida's locating the possibility of meaning in the repetition of movement between "excess" and "closed structure" whereby meanings can only be contingently and temporarily fixed, structures never totally closed and no privileged center ultimately located, which is itself stable and beyond structuring practices.

So we should not think in terms of completely open-ended multiplicities, decoded flows which elude social and political control produced by the schizophrenic pole of desire versus a fully territorialized and coded totality produced by the paranoiac pole of desire. No, these are not mutually exclusive things. The process of constructing the foundational, transcendent, overcoded structure of society, is one in which decoding, the breaking of connections, networks, and the forming of new and random ones is immanent in this very process. Underlying every code is a process of continual flux and the disruption of flux, points of contact between/among intensities.[35] Deterritorialization always has reterritorialization as its flipside. "Every code is affected by a margin of decoding."[36]

Deleuze and Guattari offer for consideration three general types of societies based on the network of desire that is implicated in their production; the primitive territorial machine, the barbarian despotic machine (the Urstaat), and the civilized capitalist machine, the latter two suggesting the most relevant insights for a theory of "the state" in the current era of globalization. With the Urstaat, the body of the socius becomes the body of the despot. The despotic state effects a movement of deterritorialization that divides the earth as an object and subjects men to the new imperial inscription, the new body, the new socius. Subjects and meanings are organized into a hierarchy beneath the king, the despot. The coded flows of the previous socius, that is, the persons, groups, lineages, alliances, filiations, rural communities, and so on find themselves overcoded by this transcendent unity that appropriates them. The old institutions remain, but are reinscribed by the state. This overcoding constitutes the essence of "the state" and measures both its continuity and its breaks with previous formations.[37] The Urstaat decodes and deterritorializes previous groupings and reterritorializes the earth making it an object of its higher unity, a forced, stratified, and overcoded aggregate. This is the paranoiac pole of desire.

While born of deterritorializing practices, "the state" itself is highly territorial. It is, however, inextricably connected to the economic processes of capitalism, which are dedicated to endless acceleration and movement bringing about the decoding of flows that the Urstaat coded and overcoded. Capitalism brings with it an assemblage of decoded flows, a new threshold of deterritorialization that overflows and overturns the previous socius, creating a new socius. Capitalism is a desiring machine.[38] It decodes and deterritorializes wealth through monetary abstraction, flows of production through merchant capital, the means of production through the formation of industrial capital, and states through financial capital. Capitalism epitomizes the schizophrenic pole of desire though significantly it only functions on condition that it inhibit its tendency to displace its own limits. Thus, along with the movement of deterritorialization is the often violent movement of reterritorialization – by no means purely a technical operation, but rather effected in various ways by formal apparatuses of the government, the forces of law and order, and an array of diverse societal forces. Reterritorialization requires "social organs of decision, administration, reaction, inscription; a technocracy and a bureaucracy that cannot be reduced to the operation of technical machines."[39] This is where statecraft comes in.

We can speak of "the state" only in a very provisional sense. It is not unitary. It is not rational. It is not an actor. It is not even a concrete "thing." Theories that insist it is these things are no more or less than powerful expressions of desire – desire for order, desire to overcome ambivalence and undecidability. That such theories are so dominant in academia and so often taken as unobjectionable, expresses a silent, collective, unconscious desire on the part of theorists that puts them on a par with government officials as practitioners of statecraft. There is no such thing as "the state," only a powerful desire for "the state" that pervades the social realm. Of course, there are governmental bureaucracies and institutions, and human subjects engaging in practices. But these, neither individually nor collectively are "the state." "The state" is nothing but a desire that is manifested in *practices of statecraft*, practices that can originate in government bureaucracies and institutions, churches, schools, corporations, theaters, novels, art museums, our backyards, our front yards, our kitchens, and living rooms and bedrooms. Practices of statecraft can come from anywhere and from anyone; from Madeline Albright to Colin Powell to young skinheads in Germany to San Diego teenagers who take sport in beating up migrant workers to vigilante ranchers on the US/Mexican border to the clerk in the local passport office. The tendency toward, but never fully accomplished concretization of "the state" is the movement of the desire for an overcoded unity. Numerous individuals and practices are implicated in this movement. "The state is desire that passes from the head of the despot to the hearts of his subjects."

Thus, the suggestion by Deleuze and Guattari that the despotic state, the Urstaat, is not one formation among others, but a regulatory ideal that "assumes its immanent concrete existence only in the subsequent forms that cause it to return under other guises and conditions."[40]

Violence in its various manifestations is at the very core of statecraft. Practices of coding and overcoding, territorializing and reterritorializing inherent to statecraft are forms of structural violence. This is not to suggest that only subjects acting on behalf of governments engage in violent practices, which of course they often do, but rather that the very concept of "the state," is an inherently violent, repressive one. Any practice of statecraft, any movement toward the never fully realized or realizable concretization of this abstract ideal is inextricably linked with violence. True, we may observe a range of practices of statecraft some tending toward an ideal we may call "democratic," some overtly despotic, fascistic and while we would not want to deny the differences in these practices, the point is that any practice of statecraft is always haunted by the model of the Urstaat, the cold monster, the nightmare. If you don't believe me, just ask Jim Auld or any of the thirteen others who were tortured by the British government, one of the most "civilized" in the world.[41] Or Joy Gardner, the Jamaican immigrant, who unfortunately can be asked nothing because she was killed after British police gagged her with more than thirteen feet of adhesive tape during an attempt to deport her.[42] Or ask Jeffrey Benzien, the South African police officer who daily left his suburban home to go to work and extract confessions with torture.[43] Or ask the family of Amadou Diallo, the unarmed, West Africa immigrant, whose body was riddled with nineteen bullets out of the forty-one total fired at him by four New York City police officers.[44] The examples go on and on, in the name of order, justified by "the state."[45] The mark of the Urstaat is apparent in these and many other diverse instances. It is perhaps more apparent in cases of overt oppression by governments, but is nonetheless present in all practices aimed at maintaining order and stability. The Urstaat raises its head at the US/Mexican border when hundreds of human beings die trying to cross at extremely dangerous points due to immigration policies such as Operation Gatekeeper.[46] It raised its head in the roundup of presumed but not in fact, "illegal aliens" in Chandler, Arizona in July of 1997.[47]

These examples should not be taken to suggest that practices of statecraft are omnipotent, only that violence pervades the desire for order that is statecraft. The fact that desire does its productive work under various social circumstances makes it open ended and unpredictable with "state violence" taking numerous forms though always presupposing the state itself. State violence, according to Deleuze and Guattari, always presents itself as pre-accomplished even though it is reactivated every day – just as the state itself appears pre-accomplished and self-presupposing.[48] "State or lawful violence always seems to presuppose itself, for it preexists its own use; the State can in this way say that violence is 'primal', that it is simply a natural phenomenon the responsibility for which does not lie with the State, which uses violence only against the violent, against 'criminals' – against primitives, against nomads – in order that peace may reign."[49]

Anti-immigrantism

Along with the deterritorializations and reterritorializations, decodings and recodings that accompany globalization, inevitably arises issues of inclusion and exclusion. Deleuze and Guattari pose the question as follows, "Are there people who are constituted in the overcoding empire, but constituted as necessarily excluded and decoded?"[50] Who is the collective figure of the outsider, the ones who do not belong, but whose constitution is inherent in the construction of the included, and the society of which they are part? For Procacci, the figure of the pauper in the nineteenth century offers a useful example of an excluded other that is itself constituted by the social order from which it is excluded.[51] Today, immigrants, legal and illegal but especially illegal, occupy an important position in the tensions discussed earlier. Constituted by the overcoding empire that is the state system, they are excluded from that system, constituted as the outside, the other, the ones whose belonging is eternally called into question. The movement of human beings across territorialized and coded geographic, cultural, and political space is itself a flow understood as threatening to order, security, and identity. It thus conjures up a broad array of reactions and practices ranging from various forms of racism to overt physical violence to practices of categorization, to the production of symbols, identities, and other meanings. Just as immigration is a significant part of globalization, anti-immigrantism is also global in nature.

Anti-immigrantism is a significant contemporary practice of statecraft and like most practices of statecraft it is motivated by a desire for order. One need only peruse a variety of publications from the United States and Europe to find numerous examples of anti-immigrantism. The *Boston Globe* reports that nativism and resentment toward immigrants is surging in Europe.[52] The *Washington Post* reports an increasingly unfriendly reception awaiting immigrants to Europe.[53] Rightist youths shout anti-immigrant insults while stabbing a man of "Asian appearance" in Guben, Germany, which was also the scene of the killing of a young Algerian last year by a xenophobic mob. Police in South London search for three white men suspected of an attack on a Turkish man that left him surviving on an artificial ventilator.[54] Jorg Haider calls for the "elimination" of all illegal immigrants living in Austria and skinheads say "What Haider can't do, we'll carry out on his behalf."[55] A region in southeastern Spain becomes the site of its worst anti-immigrant violence when several towns are overwhelmed by mobs of residents chasing Moroccan and other African immigrants through the streets, shouting racist slogans, wielding bars and sticks and thrashing foreign laborer's cars and shops.[56] The *International Herald Tribune* proclaims that "Fear of 'the Other' Fuels Rise of European Rightists."[57] Black African immigrants from Sudan and Angola suffer violence at the hands of black South Africans. At least seven foreigners were killed in xenophobic attacks across South Africa from April through August, 2000. The most dramatic incident involved two refugee brothers from Angola who were beaten up in their Cape Town home, which was then set on fire.[58]

Anti-immigrantism is not limited to these acts of overt violence and it is not necessarily the obvious forms of violence that are the most significant. Passage of California's Proposition 187, which was passed by an overwhelming majority of California voters (59 percent) in November of 1994, would be an example of a less overtly violent form of anti-immigrantism. Attempts by groups such as "U.S. English" to make English the official language of the US government can also be considered a form of anti-immigrantism. Anti-immigrantism is often present in official government practices including immigration and citizenship laws as well as border control policies. Border policies such as Operation Gatekeeper in the United States and similar ones in Europe, which push immigrants into extremely dangerous, life-threatening crossing points are also examples of anti-immigrantism. Anti-immigrantism is part of the many faceted phenomenon of globalization, perhaps an inherent feature. What has been called "the new racism" or "neo-racism" is a particularly significant aspect of anti-immigrantism. This is discussed in detail in Chapter 2.

"Methods" and cases

Play it as you would a record, say Deleuze and Guattari in *Capitalism and Schizophrenia*. "There are always cuts that leave you cold. So you skip them. Other cuts you may listen to over and over again. They follow you. You find yourself humming them under your breath as you go about your daily business."[59] I am haunted by many of Deleuze and Guattari's cuts, while I skip others. Some have left me cold, some just totally perplexed me. I rely upon much of their work for the way I understand statecraft and its relationship to desire. But I also eclectically draw from others whose words also haunt, inspire, and sometimes leave me perplexed. Foucault, Derrida, Homi Bhabha are among the thinkers who offer ideas I believe can help get at the complex array of forces and practices that characterize statecraft and produce "the state" and "the nation." I have not tried to condense or synthesize the thoughts of these people into anything resembling a coherent "methodology." Their ideas are too complicated and there is too much disagreement amongst them for that.[60] I have found elements though, from their respective works that can facilitate the understanding of statecraft I am suggesting in this study. I proceed then with a certain critical attitude gleaned from the works of these and other writers.

I have chosen to focus on three cases; the United States, Great Britain, and France. Immigration is so widespread today that nearly every rich, industrialized country has been compelled to respond to it. So, I will make no extensive arguments as to why these three cases are the absolute, essential ones that must be examined. I could have chosen many other cases with equally good reasons. That said, these three cases are significant ones and there are good reasons to study them. These three countries have all experienced significant post Second World War immigration from Third World countries. The United States, one of the world's richest countries, shares the longest border in the world with one of the poorest, Mexico and according to a recent United Nation's report has the largest intake of immigrants anywhere.[61] Mexican President, Vicente Fox's recent attention to border issues as well as the ongoing deaths of immigrants in US border crossing areas has renewed US focus on the issue of immigration. Britain was one of the earliest to experience post Second World War movements of people from former colonies and is currently the most popular destination for immigrants in Europe.[62] The issue of race, which is closely linked with immigration continues to be significant in Britain. France, like Britain, "...called for workers and there came human beings."[63] All three countries have experienced anti-immigrantism in varying forms and to varying degrees. All are ostensibly stable, highly industrialized democracies with histories of commitments to liberty, justice, equality. This is particularly important. Liberal democracies are usually understood in opposition to repressive states. However, the understanding of "the state" discussed earlier calls into question any neat opposition between democratic and repressive states. The never fully realized desire for order is an ideal that takes on many guises. It lurks within the shadows of the liberal democratic state as well as the repressive state. The United States, Britain, and France have all participated in the production and reinforcement of both external and internal borders stemming from this desire. All nicely illustrate the argument I am making about statecraft, desire, and immigration within the context of globalization.

"Method" is probably not the most appropriate word to use, conjuring as it does the specter of science and the pursuit of goals such as prediction and generalizability, which are not the goals of this study. By looking at these cases, I try to do at least three things I hope will provoke some critical reflection on contemporary practices of statecraft. First, I replace "the state" with *practices of statecraft*. While, of course I cannot completely escape this concept, which occupies so central a place in the hearts and minds and multiple discourses of academics and policy-makers, I can always surround it by quotation marks, placing it under erasure as Derrida would say, evoking ghosts of absence, the lack of foundations, the ultimately arbitrary nature of its power and authority. Clearly, I am not the first to do this and without the relentless and critical questioning of "the state" (and related concepts such as sovereignty, and nation and identity) by other students of international relations I would possibly now be thinking unreflectively in terms of unitary, rational actors patrolling the world in pursuit of absolute and relative gains or perhaps I would have just decided to go to law school or pursue an MBA. In any case, I locate this study within the critical impulses of these other scholars and hope this study will make a contribution to their own reflections.[64] Second, I offer for consideration, the concept of desire as the non-essentializable essence of statecraft, the foundationless foundation that underlies impulses of inclusion and exclusion, divisions between insides and outsides. Third, I suggest that racism is significantly implicated in contemporary practices of statecraft, that it is an expression of the desire for order, that it is a global phenomenon, that it is very much a part of international relations' practices, and should be very much a part of academic international relations.

2 Dangers and differences in a globalizing world

> Without the possibility of difference the desire of presence as such would not finds its breathing space.[1]

> The despot is threatened by any organ which breaks away from the socius and escapes overcoding.[2]

Difference is constructed along so many complex and overlapping dimensions that it would be pointless to try to reduce it to a fundamental one. A multitude of exclusionary practices have created many figures of "the other," which have enabled the effect of unambiguous, collective self-identities. Still, the inconclusiveness of such constructions, the fragility and failures of coding and territorializing practices, results in an inherent insecurity, an alertness to dangers that would undermine them. It seems that in a globalizing world these insecurities are increasingly visible.[3] In this chapter I discuss several constructions of otherness that are significant in terms of contemporary immigration practices. While I would not want to suggest that all exclusionary practices can be understood as instances of racism, "race" is inextricably connected to the constructions I focus on in this study. This can certainly be justified in view of the fact that many of the reactions to immigration from the Third World to Western industrialized countries focus on cultural differences that easily blur into constructed racial and ethnic differences.

Racism and immigration

But, how to speak of racism when we do not even know what "race" is anymore, when we are not even sure "it" is anything at all or at least anything that can be clearly defined by some set of empirical referents? It is ironic that the world is still so haunted by racism when it has become increasingly evident that there is no such thing as "race" in a genetic, biological, or scientific sense.[4] But surely we cannot ignore "race," deny its existence. Surely something is still there that echoes the word "race." We read stories of "South Africa's New Racism," which is equated with black on black xenophobia.[5] Riots in Spain against Moroccan farm workers are referred to as "racial violence."[6] An attack on Turkish asylum-seeker, Cumali Bagirtkan, in Britain is referred to as a racist attack.[7] Racial violence and anti-immigrant violence have become almost synonymous. Clearly "it" lingers, in all its vagueness, all its arbitrariness. How then to speak of "it?"

Barker suggested the term, the "new racism" to describe a new kind of racism that does not draw upon ideas of biological races that were prevalent in nineteenth-century "scientific racism." The "new racism" is a theory of human nature, which suggests that

> Human nature is such that it is natural to form a bounded community, a nation, aware of its differences from other nations. They are not better or worse. But feelings of antagonism will be aroused if outsiders are admitted. And there grows up a special form of connection between a nation and the place it lives.[8]

The "new racism," or "neo-racism," or "racism without race" is racism whose dominant theme is not biological heredity, but the insurmountability of cultural differences. Ostensibly, it does not posit the superiority of certain groups of people in relation to others, but only the harmfulness of abolishing borders, the incompatibility of life styles and traditions.[9] This kind of racism has also been referred to as "differentialist racism." In contrast to earlier forms of racism, which were legitimated by an ideology of inequality of human types, differentialist racism is "predicated on the imperative of preserving the group's identity, whose 'purity' it sanctifies."[10] The mixing of cultures is thus seen as a mistake, which endangers one's identity and can lead to social conflict. In terms of the nation and national identity, neo-racism induces an "excess of purism." For the nation to maintain its identity, to be truly itself, it must isolate and eliminate or expel "the other," the false element. This can become an obsession resulting in the racialization of social groups and the attribution to them of various qualities signifying exteriority and impurity[11] (Balibar 1991a: 59–60). Surely, the desire for presence finds its breathing space within such obsessions. Balibar suggests that neo-racism is a racism of the reversal of population movements, that is, movements from the poor "Third World" countries to the rich industrialized countries in contrast to movements in the opposite direction during the era of colonialism. To confuse neo-racism with earlier forms of racism is, according to Taguieff, a theoretical error that both inhibits our ability to understand contemporary racism and has serious consequences for struggles against racism.

Neo-racism is also a more insidious form of racism, which can be difficult to combat. It often presents itself as anti-racist, promoting the respect for differences. As Winant points out, "The struggle against racism has for nearly half a century taken the principal form of the defense of difference, of the rights of minorities, of the irreducible variety and necessary plurality of human cultures."[12] Neo-racism rearticulates this position within the context of increasing globalization in the late twentieth century and the movement of non-white peoples into Western industrialized countries.[13] It operates under the guise of the inevitability of conflict if human beings of different cultures are mixed in inappropriate numbers. It thus permits the claim to be made that exclusionary policies are actually humane, implying that conventional anti-racism is itself a cause of racism and conflict because of its failure to appreciate the laws of human nature. The significance of this phenomenon to immigration is obvious. It has been suggested that the very category of immigration has replaced that previously occupied by biological races.[14] While neo-racism draws its power from the notion of culture rather than science its effect is no less naturalizing. According to the logic of neo-racism the creation of bounded communities founded on cultural differences are a natural result of human nature. The abolition of those boundaries or the coexistence of different cultural traditions within boundaries will naturally give rise to aggression and conflict. Therefore, in order to avoid such conflict, boundaries must be reinforced. One simply must accept the laws of human nature, the tolerance thresholds that are inherent in bounded communities.

Just how new though, is the "new racism" and what is the relationship between the new and old racism or cultural versus biological racism? Certainly it is possible to find, in earlier times, instances that would contain elements of neo-racism. The "separate but equal" doctrine of the US South comes to mind. Although the justification for segregation was not cultural, ostensibly superiority on the part of whites was not claimed – only that the differences between whites and blacks should be respected.[15] Kanstroom points out that German historian, Oswald Spengler's, conception of race was beyond blood or genetics, linked more to geography and common history than biology. It was not manifested in physical characteristics but in "intangible essences." Spengler thus viewed the "Jewish question" as predominantly a cultural clash in contrast to Hitler's view of Semitic versus "Aryan" races based on blood.[16] According to Silverman the cultural underpinning of racism is not necessarily a new phenomenon, going all the way back to Ernest Renan whose answer to his own question "What is a Nation," rejected the criterion of "race" as the foundation of a nation, but introduced the equally essentialist notions of tradition and custom.[17] Manzo points out that blackness was a marker of cultural difference as the modern age approached but was always accompanied by references to factors such as customs, religion, language, and character.[18] Similarly, Goldberg argues that the cultural conception of race can be traced back to the eighteenth and nineteenth centuries.[19] Wieviorka points out that at least in the cases of Britain and Germany, the ground for race thinking was laid by the question of national unity.[20] It seems then, that culture and biology have not always been so clearly differentiated when it comes to "race" and that often questions of national identity have provided the background against which ideas regarding these were articulated. Regardless, though of whether "neo-racism" is really new, the important point is that against the background of multiple transformations brought about by globalization, it has become a significant form of contemporary racism, a way of constructing otherness that can lead to exclusion and discrimination. It occurs within the context of flows and fixations that characterize a world increasingly resistant to and at the same time preoccupied with borders. It is the widespread, dispersed quality of neo-racism today that makes it significant. Similar patterns of discourse are present throughout Europe as well as the United States.[21]

While recognizing that "neo-racism" is not necessarily new, it would certainly be equally erroneous to suggest that the old kind of racism has completely disappeared or that it is not significant in terms of anti-immigrantism. The "indicators" of "race" have historically and continue to be multiple, extremely complex, and related to one another in various ways. Brah makes this point suggesting that there is not necessarily a single neo-racism in Europe today but a variety of racisms some of which are more or less salient and which become reconstituted into new configurations.[22] Certainly, racism based on skin color still persists. What is important though is to not limit our conception of race to skin color. Taguieff cautions that to see racism only as the positing of superiority based on biological difference blinds us to the "unprecedented gentle, and euphemized forms of racism," which praise difference.[23] One could find important examples of instances in which biological racism and cultural racism become inextricably linked to one another. South Africa's apartheid system is a good example of this. Richmond suggests that the legislation and regulative institutions created to address the immigration issue in Western Europe as well as the justifications offered for them bear a remarkable similarity to those South Africa adopted to control the movement of people from outside and within its borders. South Africa's justifications included claims to racial superiority consistent with biological racism, but also justifications that are more consistent with neo-racism such as the need to preserve ethnic identity, the defense of cultural and social institutions, the obligation to limit intertribal conflict, state security, and the maintenance of law and order.[24] As will become evident in the cases examined in this study, the presumption of such laws of human nature assumed by neo-racism loom large and underlie many responses to immigration.

Peter Brimlow's *Alien Nation* is one of the more obvious examples of neo-racism and worth at least a brief look for illustrative purposes. Brimlow suggests that the "American nation has always had an ethnic core. And that core has been white." Even though, admittedly blacks constituted almost a fifth of the total population within the borders of the original thirteen colonies, most were slaves. While Brimlow does not directly condone this state of affairs, he conveniently dismisses the existence of black slaves in his definition of the core of the American nation as if the defining feature of the nation, that is, its whiteness, could be neatly separated from the physical presence within the nation's border of 20 percent of the population that was not white and not free. Of course, any such notion of a pure core requires a separation like this, a forgetting of the presence of what would disturb this claim to purity. Brimlow longingly looks back to the United States' first naturalization law in 1790, which stipulated that an applicant must be a "free white person" and to the next 175 years when the white proportion of the US population reached nearly nine-tenths of the total. Today's immigrants are, according to Brimlow, for the first time "from completely different and arguably incompatible, cultural traditions." They just happen to be non-white as well.[25] For Brimlow culture and skin color coalesce around the notion of what it means to be a true American, which for Brimlow easily translates into whiteness. The pincer whose claws are choking the American nation consists of Blacks, Asians, and Hispanics.[26]

A point that arises, at least implicitly, in Brimlow's work is the question as to in what sense can we consider the contemporary phenomenon of anti-immigrantism to be a form of racism when bias and discrimination against immigrants has been present during other periods of immigration, especially in the United States? While, as noted earlier, every instance of anti-immigrantism may not be attributable to racism, contemporary anti-immigrantism cannot be separated from the context within which it is taking place. To suggest an understanding of a prominent form of contemporary racism based on presumed cultural differences does not have to imply a fixed idea of either race or anti-immigrantism. The context that this study encompasses is one in which the source of immigrants is largely "Third World" countries with non-white populations whose destinations are Western industrialized countries with large white populations. Within such a context differences in cultural markers and differences in skin color and shades of skin color all too readily blur into one another until it may be impossible to separate them. As Hobsbawn suggests xenophobia today, all too readily shades into racism.[27] This does not necessarily imply that xenophobia has always been associated with racism in every historical setting. It does however, suggest that xenophobia today may be inextricably linked with social constructions of race and this should not be ignored.

We witness today many arguments some of which may not focus specifically on immigration but suggest the overwhelming significance of cultural differences. Samuel Huntington's widely read 1993 article is one such example. Huntington draws a sharp line between Western culture and Western ideas of individualism, liberty, equality, rule of law, democracy, and non-Western ideas that are incompatible with these and pose the potential for conflict.[28] More recently, Huntington has suggested that "migration is the central issue of our time" posing a threat to "the cultural integrity" of European countries.[29] He suggests that the United States faces the same challenge as Europe, the same potential for conflict within its domestic borders if immigration continues. According to Huntington, the assimilation of immigrants in the nineteenth century and prior to the First World War, was aided when the "waves of immigration ended" and "no more of the same kind of people came."[30] It goes without saying, for Huntington, that the meaning of the phrase "the same kind of people" is unproblematic and in no need of elaboration. His slippage from place of origin to "kinds of people" is perhaps some kind of Freudian slip, but is illustrative of neo-racism. In a recent paper published for the American Enterprise Institute Huntington considers "The Special Case of Mexican Immigration."[31] Huntington makes the distinction between "immigrants" and "settlers" suggesting that the "Early Americans did not immigrate to an existing society; they established new societies." This distinction enables Huntington to dismiss, erase, make invisible inhabitants prior to European settlers. As with Brimlow, the purity of the American core requires such an erasure. The United States was an uninhabited blank, slate upon which American identity, culture, and greatness could be written. According to Huntington, "Mexican immigration looms as a unique and disturbing challenge to our cultural integrity, our national identity, and potentially to our future as a country."[32]

Michael Walzer offers another example of anxiety over the mixing of cultures. "Neighborhoods can be open only if countries are at least potentially closed .... The distinctiveness of cultures and groups depends upon closure and, without it, cannot be conceived as a stable feature of human life ...."[33] For Brimlow, Huntington, and Walzer the blurring of sharp lines that would differentiate cultures and peoples are moments of anxiety that portend potentially dire consequences. The despot is threatened by that which escapes overcoding. When put into a larger context of the increasingly blurred nature of national borders, the movement of people across these borders, the evermore restrictive immigration and refugee policies enacted by the Western world, and the linkages between culture and "race," these discourses can certainly be understood as, at the very least, part of the myriad of enabling conditions for neo-racism.[34] They participate in the naturalization and justification of exclusionary practices based on presumed and essentialized cultural identities. While admittedly Walzer seems to recognize that cultural differences are not inherent but rather dependent on exclusions, he simultaneously justifies those exclusions as necessary for distinguishing among cultures and groups, a distinction he deems inherently desirable.[35]

To summarize and reiterate, the presumption I begin with is that "race" is a social construct.[36] It has no inherent or fixed meaning. What "race" is emerges within specific historical, economic, and political situations and is whatever racists have the social power to define it as. It is an open-ended political category constituted out of struggle.[37] The concept of neo-racism directs our attention to the construction of race within the context of late twentieth-century globalization and its implications for national boundaries and the politics of inclusion and exclusion. It is vital in understanding how race is implicated in the processes by which boundaries, divisions, and national identities are constructed and reconstructed. It has the capacity to link the issues of national identity, immigration, xenophobia, and various forms of exclusion which give race one of its contemporary meanings. Neo-racism is important in understanding the forms of exclusion that are particularly relevant to immigration, the insecurities connected with immigration and the accompanying desire for order and security. Neo-racism results from the overcoding practices that attempt to counter the decoding and deterritorialization that is inherent in contemporary immigration. Neo-racism functions as a supplement to the nationalism that arises from the blurring of boundaries and the problemetizing of national identity that the deterritorialization of human bodies gives rise to. Balibar suggests that racism is always in excess of nationalism, "but always indispensable to its constitution and yet always still insufficient to achieve its project."[38] The desire for order is manifested in neo-racism's attempts to obliterate the ambiguity regarding national identity that accompanies the movement and settlement of human beings across geopolitical boundaries. To highlight the phenomenon of neo-racism should not however, be taken to suggest that more conventional forms of racism are not still at work or that other forms of exclusion are not present. The immigration issue, in fact, illustrates that various exclusionary practices are often at work simultaneously and that conventional racism and other forms of exclusion can work together.

Strangers, paupers, and Third World immigrants

There are dimensions other than racial and cultural ones that have been important in constructing difference, in distinguishing "others" from selves and that are significant in the construction of nation-states. The idea of the nation has always entailed an alertness to "false elements," the ones who do not belong. As this idea was emerging along with the related notions of citizenship and the rights it entailed, the concept of the foreigner was being produced juridically, administratively, and ideologically. For example, Silverman suggests that it was the expansion of the state that accompanied rapid industrialization in France during the nineteenth century that provided the foundation for the emergence of a particular understanding of "the foreigner."[39] Similarly, Enloe suggests the significance of state-building and expansion in the United States for the distinction between its subjects and "aliens."[40] Statecraft has been and is inextricably linked with "the other." In this section I examine two figures of "the other" that are not necessarily new or specific to Third World immigrants in Western societies, nor inherently connected to racism. However, these two figures of "the other" come together in constructions of the Third World immigrant and become linked with contemporary racisms. These two figures are the stranger and the pauper.

The borders that separate national, state controlled spaces, and the conceptual demarcations that mark the opposition between the inside of this space and the outside beyond it are disrupted by the figure of the stranger. Neither friend nor foe, the stranger is inherently unde-cidable. Physically close yet remote, the stranger is a constant threat to the spatial ordering of the world. The stranger is at the margins, always already decoded and deterritorialized, ineradicably ambiva-lent. Today in the late twentieth century there are many strangers in the world. Strangers in the form of immigrants (legal and illegal) and refugees are dispersed throughout the world calling into question established spatial images of domesticity versus anarchy and chaos, giving rise to intense desires for order and stability and an easily iden-tifiable community. The massive movements of peoples across geo-graphic, political, and social borders and the consequences of such movements unravels the single braid that international relations the-ory weaves around the conceptual space of "the state." The concep-tual demarcation between the inside and the outside becomes contaminated, the unity of the nation-state questioned. The natural, taken for granted nature of these divisions is threatened.[41] While these divisions have never been fully fixed, totally coded and territorialized, their arbitrary, fragile, and contingent nature arguably becomes more profoundly so during times when decoded and deterritorialized flows become more numerous and widespread. Strangers, those constituted as other to the national self become more visible and are seen as more threatening. Practices of codification and territorialization proliferate.

Georg Simmel's definition of the stranger as one who comes today and stays tomorrow, that is, the notion that the stranger's stay is in some sense permanent or at least long term and thus cannot be ignored, is pertinent.[42] This is indeed what creates tension blurring the lines between the domestic realm of order and the outside realm of insecurity. While the stranger is spatially on the inside, his/her position is fundamentally affected by the fact that he/she is not constituted as indigenous to the inside though his/her constitution is inextricably linked to the constitution of the inside. Kristeva suggests that the stranger (or the foreigner) lives within us, the hidden face of our identity, a symptom that turns "we" into a problem.[43] While the stranger is spatially on the inside, his/her very presence defies the easy expedient of spatial segregation. The stranger is defined a priori as a challenge to the clarity of the world and thus to the authority of reason. The stranger cannot but call into question most of the things the natives take as unquestionable.[44] The stranger is thus a threat to the social order.

The figure of the pauper is another social figure that has been deemed disruptive to the social order. The discourse of pauperism arose in the first half of the nineteenth century. It was articulated by the social economists who suggested that in order to enable the wealth-producing mechanisms of the economy to work, it was not enough to remove the obstacles of obsolete privileges and the restrictive policies of mercantilism.[45] Pauperism came to signify the "ensemble of adversities/adversaries which confront the project of social order."[46] It was not poverty *per se* that the discourse on pauperism was directed toward. Rather, the discourse on pauperism took as its object of attack, difference. Pauperism signified a series of conducts, a set of physical and moral habits that were deemed antithetical to the social order. The discourse on pauperism drew upon images of indefiniteness, fluidity, and mobility. "Pauperism is mobility: against the need for territorial sedentarization, for fixed concentration of population, it personified the residue of a more fluid, elusive sociality, impossible either to control or to utilize."[47] The personality and mentality of economic man cannot be implanted among the populations of the poor except as a broader strategy, a political technology designed to form, out of the recalcitrant material of the "dangerous classes," something more than economic man; a social citizen.[48] The cluster of behaviors, the natural appetites that were deemed obstacles to the construction of the social citizen then had to be channeled and guided so as to "aspire to find their satisfaction through the means permitted them by the social regime."[49]

The figure of the stranger and the figure of the pauper come together in contemporary times in the figure of the non-European, Third World immigrant. Like the stranger and the pauper the immigrant has been frequently constituted as a danger to the social order. Responses vary, but all seek to combat disorder, to overcome ambivalence, to recode and reterritorialize, to reassert and reconstruct identities and criteria of belonging, to reassert the unity of the nation-state. These attempts come from various directions but, all are illustrative of the desire for order. All are practices of inscribing meanings and identities in those ambivalent spaces between the inside and the outside, between order and disorder, between clarity and ambiguity. They are, in a word, practices of statecraft. Today's immigrant is both stranger and pauper, simultaneously constituted by the social order, and deemed a threat to it.

Statecraft and the other(s)

Immigration is one of the contemporary sites of statecraft and one where neo-racism is seriously implicated. Homi Bhabha's ideas are useful for understanding how this process works, particularly his ideas on the contradictory and ambivalent structure of colonial discourse and the construction of a national "people" in double time. The construction of the immigrant like that of the stranger and the pauper is quite similar to the construction of the colonial subject in terms of the logic at work. In analyzing colonial discourse Bhabha directs attention to the conflictual positions that constitute the subject in order to show the occurrence of a slippage, which problematizes any notion of a single position on the part of the colonizer as well as any instrumental relation between power and knowledge in constituting the colonial subject. He suggests that the mastery of colonial discourse is always asserted, but always slipping, always being displaced, and never finally completed. The stability of colonial discourse and the categories and identities it constructs is "continually under threat from diachronic forms of history and narrative, signs of instability."[50] Similarly, the construction of the internal of the nation-state is characterized by a continual slippage between the desire for the pedagogical, the given, self-evident presence of unity and order and the performative, always in process negotiation with flows, flux, and movement, which resists coding. "The people" are constituted in this double time. The nation and "the state" that represents it gain their authority by virtue of a desire for the pedagogical. The paranoiac pole of desire works toward the production of the pedagogical.

Statecraft always takes place in this double time where the pedagogical is continually intervened in and contested by the performative, the schizophrenia pole of desire. The performative introduces a gap or emptiness to the signifier by casting a shadow between it and the signified. For example, illegal immigration introduces such a gap in that it is no longer so clear just what the signifier "domestic" refers to. The presence of strangers casts a shadow between what is on the one hand signified by the assumptions of sovereign, territorial borders, neatly enclosed nation-states, and on the other hand the absence of concrete signifieds that would attest to the validity of these assumptions. Deleuze and Guattari refer to assignifying signs that deliver themselves over to the order of desire, that is, the signs themselves become deterritorialized and lose the minimum conditions of identity that define the signifier.[51] Practices of statecraft move ambivalently between the pedagogical and the performative toward a re-establishment of the conditions of identity. It is in this sense that statecraft is characterized by a double-writing, which both produces the givenness of the nation-state and those who belong on the inside, but simultaneously produces the strangers, the excluded, which destabilize the inside.

The immigrant as a danger to the social order is constituted in the interstices of the tensions between the two and becomes an important focal point around which the tensions are managed.[52]

Bauman outlines several responses to strangers that have been operative historically and that continue in contemporary times.[53] The effect of these has been to channel, recode, and reterritorialize the flow of human beings that traverse geographic space that itself has been coded and territorialized. I think of these as *realms of territorialization* and draw upon some of them for the analysis of the responses to post Second World War immigration in the cases that make up this study. I discuss these briefly below and in more detail in the following chapters.

The most extreme response is to force the strangers to leave and thereby re-establish the original and unambivalent social order. Policies that are obviously consistent with this are deportations and restrictions on immigration. Maintaining control of geographic space by keeping strangers on the other side of the border helps to construct and perpetuate a myth of purity, when the outside was unambiguously differentiated from the inside. Andreas notes that far from disappearing, many borders are being reasserted and remade through ambitious and innovative state efforts to regulate the transnational movement of people. The size of the US border patrol alone has more than doubled since 1993.[54] Equally significant though is the rhetoric that revolves around the border. The border, for all of its ambivalence, is still a powerful symbol of the line that separates strangers from those who truly belong. The rhetoric itself is a practice of statecraft that may or may not actually result in the strangers leaving but nonetheless functions to reinforce the notion of an inside versus an outside.

Cultural fences and ethnic ghettos are ways of containing and separating strangers from non-strangers when forcing them to leave is not feasible.[55] Richmond also refers to "distancing" and separation that is imposed by a dominant group on a less powerful one, apartheid being one of the most well-known and recent examples.[56] We can think of these kinds of practices as examples of the "exteriorization of the interior." The linking of various social ills such as crime and disease to immigrants as well as the denial of rights enjoyed by citizens would also fall under this category of response. It is within this complex process of exteriorizing aspects of the interior that the territorial border is supplemented by the production of internal boundaries that are themselves always unstable, contingent, and ambivalent. It is at these sites of exteriorization that practices of statecraft shift to the spaces in which governments negotiate their relationships with, and indeed define who is to be included within, civil society. In an important sense borders themselves become deterritorialized and decoded flows, moving inward transgressing the very assumption that there is a clear and fixed boundary between the inside and the outside. Domestic governmental policies function to recode and reterritorialize those borders and in the process to code the internal "other," the internal stranger.

Finally, we have responses that fall under the headings of integration and assimilation. Integration and assimilation have been prominent themes in nearly all of the Western industrialized countries experiencing post Second World War immigration. Ostensibly the assimilation of immigrants into the social, cultural, and political life of a host country would seem to entail the obliteration of stranger status. However, as has been pointed out, assimilation is itself full of contradictions and ambivalence, revealing an inner contradiction that is central to modernity itself.[57] Assimilation is a one-directional process that reaffirms the superiority of those to whom the stranger must assimilate. It reveals the tension inherent in the universalism and particularism dichotomy. Derrida's discussion of exemplarity is relevant here. Assimilation promotes the inscription of the universal in the singular. The value of universality is linked to the value of exemplarity that "inscribes the universal in the proper body of a singularlity, of an idiom or a culture, whether this singularity be individual, social, national, state," and so on. "Whether it takes a national form or not, a refined, hospitable or aggressively xenophobic form or not, the self-affirmation of an identity always claims to be responding to the call or assignation of the universal."[58] Silverman suggests that "assimilation seeks to fix the other just as much as racial determinism."[59]

Inclusionary policies such as integration and assimilation then, are not so unambiguously benign in that the presumptions that underlay them are often similar to the presumptions that underlay exclusionary policies. Policies of dispersal that are found in many countries dealing with immigrants and refugees occupy a space somewhere between containment and integration. Dispersal policies seek to prevent large numerical concentrations of immigrants in any one area. The desirability of assimilation is often cited as a reason. Inherent in all of these responses however, is the presumption of an other or others whose differences are potentially disruptive of the social/political order and therefore must be eliminated. Richmond points out that many considerations that Western countries take into account when enacting policies that restrict immigrant and refugee movement, are not necessarily racist in themselves. However, in assuming that controls are a necessary precondition for social harmony, restrictive policies implicitly label non-white immigrants as less desirable and provide a legitimation, however spurious, for racist attitudes.[60] Thus, enabled is the categorization of human beings in which neo-racism is all too often implicated and inextricably linked to national identity. Third World immigrants, strangers, paupers – their characteristics merge into one another, all become a threat to order.

3 Mark your territory

Introduction

> What is clear is that globalization also means people moving around in ways which are more constant, fluid and massive than before. This is not new. But obviously the quantities and the impact on societies is growing. We think that people who are strong advocates of globalization in some areas should be advocates of it in all areas, because there is not a lot they can do about it.[1]

> To code desire – and the fear, the anguish of decoded flows – is the business of the socius. Society is not first of all a milieu for exchange where the essential would be to circulate or to cause to circulate, but rather a socius of inscription where the essential thing is to mark and be marked.[2]

Nowhere is the tension between boundary defying forces of globalization and the desire for order more manifest than in the issue of immigration in the United States. The tensions are not new. They have been present at various times, even before the term "globalization" was so widely used. They were obvious in the near unanimous approval of the Immigration and Financial Responsibility Act of 1996 by Senators who were well aware of the appeal of promising to crack down on illegal immigration, but also equally aware that they owed their seats to the patronage of manufacturing and agribusiness interests "desirous of nothing so much as a low minimum wage and unfettered access to cheap nonunion labor from the Third World."[3] In her study of the Bracero Program, Calavita noted the contradiction between the importance of immigrants (legal as well as illegal) as a source of much needed cheap labor and the fact that this labor is attached to human beings.[4] Kearney suggests that the task of effective immigration policy is to disembody the labor from the migrant worker. "Foreign labor is desired, but the persons in whom it is embodied are not desired."[5]

The conflicting desires these writers refer to resonate with the tensions discussed in Chapter 1; the flows and deterritorializations of globalization on the one hand and the practices that seek to codify and manage these flows on the other. It is becoming increasingly difficult to successfully manage the contradictions embedded in the immigration issue in the United States as these tensions are manifested in current debates on amnesty for illegal immigrants and a guest worker program.[6] The schizophrenic nature of statecraft arguably reaches its pinnacle in border control policies that simultaneously push immigrants to their deaths at dangerous crossing points and then attempt to rescue them.[7] Border deaths are at least partially responsible for the widespread attention currently being given to immigration, particularly guest worker proposals. In this chapter I focus on the related issues of illegal immigration and the demand for the labor of this population and the rights or lack thereof afforded immigrants, legal and illegal. It should be noted that in reality legal and illegal immigration cannot so unproblematically be separated. This is especially the case when it comes to immigrants' rights. Efforts to deal with illegal immigration often have significant effects on those immigrants who are here legally. Much of the concern over immigration, in general, stems from initial concerns over illegal immigration. The issues of immigrants and immigrant labor are illustrative of how practices of statecraft oscillate between the two poles of desire discussed in Chapter 1.

The urstaat, democracy, and immigration

Much more than a physical marker that differentiates the territorial space of one nation-state from that of another, the border itself is often a flow, moving along with those whose identities have been marked with odious terms such as "illegal alien" or the current acronym of preference, UDA (undocumented alien). The geographic border is supplemented by the production of internal borders. Reterritorializing practices shift to those spaces where domestic manifestations of the desire for order collide with the impulses of a liberal, democratic state and the necessities of a globalized, capitalist world. Two pieces of legislation passed in 1996 represent the harshest crackdown on immigrants' rights in recent years and exemplify the desire for order, to once and for all distinguish "us" from "them," and to exclude "them" from the privileges that belong only to "us."[8] The Illegal Immigration Reform and Immigrant Responsibility Act of 1996 and the Personal Responsibility and Work Opportunity

Reconciliation Act of 1996 departed significantly from previous legislation in their overwhelmingly exclusionary nature, their restriction of rights and benefits granted to immigrants, and the deepening of the differences between citizens and non-citizens.[9] In the words of Republican Senator, Alan Simpson, "We have stuff in there that has everything but the rack and thumbscrews for people who are violating the laws of the United States."[10]

The Illegal Immigration Reform and Immigrant Responsibility Act of 1996 made entry into the United States significantly more difficult, mandating the construction of a triple-tiered fence and system of roads along the border near San Diego and increasing the number of Border Patrol agents by 1,000 per year for the next five years.[11] This fortification of the border pushed the Border Patrol's parent organization, the Immigration and Naturalization Service (INS), ahead of the FBI as the nation's largest federal law enforcement agency. As of 1998 the INS had more than 15,000 officers authorized to carry weapons and make arrests, which was more than the FBI, the Bureau of Prisons, the Customs Service, or the Drug Enforcement Administration.[12] Representative Lamar Smith, Chairman of the House Judiciary Subcommittee on Immigration, at the time, said that the new law "is securing America's borders, reducing crime, protecting jobs and saving taxpayers' billions of dollars."[13]

The 1996 Act, was not the first (or the last) piece of legislation to make unauthorized border crossing more difficult, nor have such border reinforcements been limited to the San Diego area. Operation Gatekeeper was launched in 1994 and initially focused on 5 miles of Imperial Beach that accounted for nearly 25 percent of all illegal border crossings nationwide. Gatekeeper was later expanded to cover the entire 66 miles of border under the San Diego Sector's jurisdiction. The model for Operation Gatekeeper was Operation Hold the Line, which was initiated in the El Paso Sector in 1993 and produced a 50 percent decline in apprehensions from FY 1993 to FY 1996. In 1995, Operation Safeguard was launched in Nogales, Arizona. It more than tripled the number of border patrol agents in the region, from 300 in the years before FY 1994 to over 1,000 by August, 2000.[14] In 1999, Operation Safeguard was expanded to the Tucson Sector which includes Naco and Douglas, Arizona.[15]

The lucky ones who survive the trek across the border face the prospect of deportation and/or detention. The aspect of the 1996 Act dealing with deportation went into effect on April 1, 1997. Asylum-seekers who arrive at an airport or other port of entry with false or no documents and seek asylum on the grounds of religious or political persecution are given an on the spot interview by a low-level immigration officer without the benefit of attorneys or translators. If the immigration officer does not believe their story they will be immediately deported. They have the opportunity to contest such a decision by requesting an administrative review by an immigration judge, which must be completed within seven days. During this time the refugee is held in detention. Those who do not claim to be fleeing persecution may be deported immediately without administrative hearing or judicial review. Even those judged to be legitimate refugees will not be eligible for asylum if they can be sent to a third country where their life or freedom will not be threatened and with which the United States has a bilateral agreement. In addition the 1996 Act states that individuals shall be detained if their identity cannot be discovered.

Amin Al-Torfi knows about the vagaries of the asylum process, as does Mohamed Jama Abdille and Patrick Mkhizi and thousands of other asylum-seekers who are held in detention. Amin arrived at Kennedy Airport on August 31, 2000 after an eighteen-month journey from southern Iraq. Because it is nearly impossible for an Iraqi citizen to get a passport or visa, he traveled with a false Canadian passport. Amin was arrested at the airport and taken to a detention center run by a private prison company, where he remained for five months.[16] Mohamed Jama Abdille sought asylum after fleeing Somalia. Even though a judge believed his tale of torture he was jailed in the United States for twenty-one months.[17] Patrick Mkhizi, son of an opponent of former President Mobuto Sese Seko of what was then Zaire, won asylum in the United States after three years in INS custody. He fled the Democratic Republic of Congo (formerly Zaire) in 1997 after Mobuto's soldiers stormed into his family's hut.[18]

Judicial review was severely curtailed by the 1996 Immigration Act. Through a process of "expedited removal" immigration officials can quicky deport asylum-seekers and illegal immigrants who show up at the border and at airports. Immigration officials, not judges determine who can be deported. Unless asylum-seekers can prove a credible fear to immigration officials upon arrival, they are not granted appearance before an immigration judge. The courts are prohibited from holding the INS accountable for its decisions in almost every discretionary area except discretionary grants of asylum. Courts may not hold the INS accountable in final orders of deportation. As of February, 2001 deportations had gone up by 164 percent. More than 721,000 immigrants, legal and illegal had been removed since the 1996 law went into effect.[19]

Those already in the United States, accused of having entered the country within the past two years illegally are treated as if they were just arriving at the border. Constitutional safeguards of due process are subject to the "summary exclusion" imposed on those just arriving. Those who stay in the United States beyond the expiration date of their temporary visa or who have entered without inspection by the INS for more than 180 days, but less than one year, are barred from reentering the United States for three years. Those who are unlawfully present in the United States for one year or more are barred from reentering for ten years.[20] The 1996 Act also expanded the definition of deportable crimes and directed the INS to deport immigrants convicted of crimes even if they are permanent and legal residents of the United States. The law took away the discretionary power of judges who in the past were able to consider mitigating factors before issuing orders of deportation. A third law, the Antiterrorism and Effective Death Penalty Act, specified a broad range of offenses for which immigrants would be ineligible to seek a waiver of deportation.[21]

It is significant that the 1996 immigration legislation took place within the context of the downsizing of social services, a rollback of state welfare policies. The Personal Responsibility and Work Opportunity Act of 1996 had important ramifications for legal immigrants. For the first time legal immigrants were barred from receiving most federal means tested public benefits including SSI and food stamps. Immigrants legally entering the United States on or after August 22, 1996 were also barred from receiving these benefits as well as Temporary Assistance for Needy Families (formerly AFDC) for the first five years.[22] The 1996 welfare reform barred those categorized as "not qualified aliens" from most federal, state, and local public benefits. The term "not qualified" refers to undocumented immigrants and others with temporary authority to remain in the United States. The types of public benefits from which they are barred included health, disability, public or assisted housing, post-secondary education, food assistance, unemployment benefits, or any similar benefit for which payment or assistance is provided to an individual, household, or family unit by an agency of the US state or local government or by appropriated funds of the US state, or local government.[23] Service providers are required to verify that those applying for federal public benefits are qualified aliens.

Nearly half of the $54 billion in estimated savings from welfare reform was expected to come from the immigrant exclusions.[24] It is important to note that the research on welfare use among immigrants is far from conclusive. Research findings regarding the number of immigrants using welfare vary a great deal due to disagreements among researchers about which programs to count as welfare and whom to classify as an immigrant.[25] For example, some researchers focus on households and consider a household to be an immigrant household if the head of the household is an immigrant. Others suggest that using the household as the unit of analysis tends to inflate immigrant welfare participation rates because 67 percent of immigrant-headed household contain a native-born person and 52 percent contain a native-born child.[26]

The Urban Institute finds that the differences in welfare participation rates between native-born US citizens and immigrants is due largely to refugees and elderly immigrants. Specifically, it finds high rates of welfare use on the part of refugees and high rates of SSI and Medicaid use on the part of elderly immigrants. It finds virtually no immigrant-native differences among working-age, non-refugee immigrants in any means tested program.[27] It is not, of course, the purpose of this study to enter into this debate on relative numbers or classifications. I bring it up here to point out that research results are not straightforward and the very existence and importance of this research points to a preoccupation with determining who belongs and who does not. This is, as discussed earlier, an important practice of statecraft. Given the borderless nature of the economy, how is the task of a governable order to be fulfilled? Who is to be entitled to social protection? The issue of welfare and other benefits for immigrants arises within this context.

Foucault's writings on governmentality and Polanyi's writings on social protection both presumed unproblematic boundaries between the inside and outside of societies, the domestic and the international. Both implicitly conceived of domestic society as unambiguously bounded and differentiated from the international. The issue of governmentality does not go away though when unproblematic boundaries can no longer be presumed. Arguably it becomes even more complicated when such a presumption cannot be easily made. The tensions discussed in Chapter 1 become globalized. An essential practice of governmentality then is to reterritorialize the spaces within which social protection and rights are to be granted, to draw the boundaries between those to be included and those to be excluded, in other words to make a show of marking one's territory. The 1996 legislation assigns identities and thereby creates internal borders that are arguably as significant as the geographical borders that differentiate states from one another.

The "exteriorization of the interior" is a significant aspect of practices of statecraft in constructing the identities of those who belong and those who do not. The 1996 welfare reform transforms the meaning of citizenship, representing a fundamental redefinition of immigrants' membership in society. Legal immigrants and their families are singled out for harsher treatment than other poverty populations. Fix and Zimmerman suggest that welfare reform may represent the most important redefinition of citizenship since the Fourteenth Amendment. Still, immigration numbers have not been reduced and immigration continues to be primarily for the purpose of family reunion.[28] This fact coupled with the two 1996 pieces of legislation are illustrative of the contradictory nature of statecraft. The various practices of marking one's territory does not necessarily result in clearer and more secure borders. Rather it effects the designation of enemies and the marginalization and repression of certain peoples.

"Citizenship stripping" and raids on certain "foreign looking" populations are practices of statecraft that function to perpetuate a myth of purity whereby various social ills can be attributed to those that do not really belong, those who are not part of the basic ethnic core as articulated by Brimlow, those who are not "us," even when they are physically and legally present. The 1996 immigration reform gave the INS the power to conduct administrative hearings to strip citizenship from newly naturalized immigrants, a power that until then had resided with the courts.[29] As of July 15, 1998 the INS had moved to strip the citizenship of almost 1,700 people under the power of administrative hearings. The desire for order and purity is also at work in practices such as requests for identification from persons of "foreign appearance," the Chandler, Arizona roundup being an exemplary case. What has become known as "the roundup" was a five-day operation in July of 1997, which targeted scores of legal residents, and US citizens in an effort to capture suspected illegal immigrants in downtown Chandler, Arizona. Chandler police officers teamed up with INS agents and arrested 432 suspected illegal immigrants. In the process many native born and legalized Mexican immigrants were pulled aside, questioned, and asked to prove their citizenship. The raid was part of Operation Restoration, which began in July, 1997. Two dozen Chandler police and five Border Patrol agents fanned out across Chandler's downtown. People were questioned leaving work sites, in their homes, and leaving markets patronized by Latinos (who make up 15 percent of Chandler's population). Venecia Robles Zavala was stopped and asked for papers as she left the "Food 4 Less" market with her children. The officer only let her go after she found a copy of her birth certificate in her car. The raid in Chandler, Arizona was one of dozens of similar actions taken by authorities in Southwestern and Rocky Mountain boomtowns.[30]

Legal raids also occur for the purpose of enforcing the Illegal Immigration and Reform Responsibility Act, which requires the INS to deport non-US citizens who have been convicted of aggravated felonies in the United States. In 1998, the Board of Immigration Appeals ruled that, for immigration purposes, a felony conviction for driving while intoxicated (DWI) is an aggravated felony. In September 1998, Operation Last Call was conducted in Texas in which 530 legal immigrants who had been convicted of felony drunk driving were arrested. In many cases the violations had taken place long ago and many of those convicted had reformed and were supporting US citizen families. Whether these practices actually result in physically removing people, internal borders are created; internal "others" constructed.

Labor – do not attempt to win the game

Deleuze and Guattari use the concept of nomadism in an attempt to capture the idea of shifting boundaries, scrambled codes, and deterritorialized space. Nomadism involves any activity that transgresses contemporary social codes through the dissolution of cultural and territorial boundaries. It often works as a form of indirect opposition to "the state."[31] Illegal immigration is a modern form of nomadism, transgressing the legal and social codes that designate bodies as belonging or not belonging to particular nation-states. When people move illegally across state boundaries, the striated, bounded nature of that space becomes smooth and open ended. Nomadism and nomadic subjects are threats to the coded unity of modern nation-states. The desire for order prompts the reterritorialization of nomadic space. However, state desire operates within a social space that is also inhabited by the schizophrenic desire of capitalism. "It is thus proper to State deterritorialization to moderate the super deterritorializations of capital and to provide the latter with commpensatory reterritorializations."[32]

This continual oscillation between deterritorialization and reterritorialization is increasingly evident in the relationship between the desirability of labor and the undesirability of the human beings to which it is attached. The schizophrenic nature of statecraft is exemplified in the elaborate US border game whose goal is not necessarily to win, but to "hide your losses" and "return all captured pawns to the board."[33] Despite the popular perception that immigrants are drawn to the United States partly because of its social assistance programs, there is no credible evidence to support this. Rather, the evidence suggests that immigrants are attracted to the United States because of perceived economic opportunities.[34] It is also increasingly obvious that immigrant labor, particularly that of illegal immigrants is a significant part of the US economy.[35]

Deleuze and Guattari speak of "neo-territorialities" that result from the reterritorializing of nomadic space. These neoterritorialities take many forms ranging from urban gangs to Indian reservations. They are often artificial, residual, archaic, and represent social and potentially political forces.[36] Illegalities, such as illegal immigration, which is actually promoted by and the result of statecraft results in a type of neo-territory. Illegal immigrant workers, "UDAs", can be thought of as a type of neo-territory not necessarily linked to a particular geographic space, a "floating population" akin to paupers in the nineteenth century. They are simultaneously useful and a perceived threat to the social order. Referring to the discourse on pauperism in the nineteenth century, Procacci suggests that "This floating population of the great cities... which industry attracts and is unable to regularly employ... is an object of serious attention and disquiet for both thinkers and governments. And it is among its ranks that pauperism is recruited, that dangerous enemy of our civilization."[37] Pauperism was poverty intensified to the level of social danger.

The figure of the pauper in the first half of the nineteenth century bears a significant resemblance to the figure of the illegal immigrant in the United States today. Images of pauperism stressed feelings of fluidity and indefiniteness, conveying the impression, at once massive and vague. It was a composite population, which encircled the social order from within, from its tenements, its industrial agglomerations. It was a magma in which was fused all the dangers, which beset the social order, shifting along unpredictable, untraceable channels of transmission and aggregation.[38] Several weapons were used to combat pauperism, most of which would be considered inclusive, for example, mutual aid societies, insurance, and education. All were for the purpose of simultaneously stabilizing individuals and breaking down the old systems of kinship, but also functioned as a polymorphous social instrument, which enabled different members to be played off against each other.[39] The different classifications of immigrants that is emphasized in the previous section on the 1996 legislation, while for the most part exclusionary in nature, also illustrate the way immigrants are divided from and played off against each other.

This is most evident in the differentiation between illegal and legal immigrants and illegal immigrants and asylum-seekers. While many are opposed to the denial of various rights to legal immigrants and legitimate refugees, there seems to be an unspoken acceptance that illegal immigrants are not entitled to rights. This is implied in the very concept of illegality.[40] In reality illegal and legal immigration are inextricably intertwined, with both coming primarily for the purposes of work, via established networks of family and friends and both living in the same neighborhoods and households.[41] However, the differentiation between legal and illegal immigrant may in fact be functional as Dunn has suggested, serving as an obstacle to solidarity between native-born workers and immigrants, thus erecting fences around those deemed illegal.[42] Constable notes how the illegality of immigrants identifies their status as persons to be one of exclusion from the political sphere of rights whereas illegality when referring to citizens or legal residents refers to specific acts and not the person.[43] The frequent synonymous use of the terms illegal immigrant and undocumented worker also suggests the relegation of individuals so classified to the sphere of work and labor and their exclusion from the sphere of rights. However, there is often a slippage between the categories of illegal immigrant and legal immigrant. Both get constructed as "other" to those who naturally belong and become associated with a host of social dangers and disorders such as crime, drug trafficking, and terrorism.

As the processes and effects of global capitalism are increasingly deterritorialized and the boundaries between nation-states become ever more porous, immigrant labor, particularly that which is embodied in those who cross borders illegally is desirable for several reasons. Reterritorializing this labor as the "illegal immigrant" problem is functional in the sense that it separates it from the category of legal immigration and permits the playing off against each other discussed above. Illegal immigrants are today's paupers, the dangerous population that cannot be assimilated into society. At a minimum this is functional in an economic sense. This is especially evident in the area of farm workers. California growers have depended on low cost illegal immigrant labor for decades. A University of California Berkeley study, released in December 1998, reported that the proportion of California farm laborers working illegally has soared in the 1990s from about 9 percent in 1990–1991 to 42 percent in 1995–1997. Three-quarters of the workers earn less than $10,000 annually.[44] According to a General Accounting Office report released in early 1998, about 40 percent of all farm workers in the United States are in the country illegally. In California, some farm owners say that number is closer to 70 percent. Manual farm labor is, at least initially, cheaper than mechanical harvesters and pruners.[45] A more recent study estimates that 58 percent of crop workers are "unauthorized" immigrants.[46]

The meatpacking industry is another area that is heavily dependent on immigrant labor. The ambiguous distinction between illegal and legal immigrants as well as the schizophrenic nature of enforcement is well illustrated by the case of IBP Inc., the largest meatpacking company in the United States with slaughterhouses in Nebraska, Kansas, and Indiana. IBP recruits workers in Mexican towns such as Fresnillo, a poor mining town in central Mexico. Starting pay at IBP is 8 dollars per hour plus medical and dental insurance. IBP says it cannot keep its plants fully staffed with American workers. Mexican workers are attractive because they work for relatively cheap wages, demand few benefits, and are generally impervious to union-organizing efforts. The INS raided IBP's plants six times between 1994 and 1997, most recently arresting 142 workers at a single slaughterhouse. However, a new program called "Basic Pilot," which helps companies verify green-card and Social Security numbers of new employees has virtually eliminated INS roadblocks for IBP. Basic Pilot was created as part of the 1996 Immigration Reform Act under pressure from anti-immigrant forces. In return, companies are virtually free from INS raids. Critics and union officials such as the United Food and Commercial Workers union say this Basic Pilot has permitted IBP to import cheap labor.[47] No IBP plant has been raided by the INS since the company joined the Basic Pilot in October 1997.[48] Basic Pilot is a good example of the ambivalent nature of immigration enforcement. Arguably the program functions so as to facilitate the continued hiring of cheap immigrant labor, as union officials suggest. It is a performative practice, which while drawing upon the presumption of and desire for clear and unambiguous borders, actually reinforces the fundamental ambiguity between who belongs and who does not.

As noted in the opening to this chapter, this ambiguity comes to the fore in contemporary proposals and debates on amnesty for illegal immigrants and an expanded guest worker program. In a historic move, the AFL–CIO has joined Mexico in calling for legal status for illegal immigrant workers.[49] Mexico insists that any border agreement with the United States must include legalization of the 3–4 million undocumented Mexican citizens already living in the United States.[50] Guest worker programs illustrate the simultaneous participation in the deterritorialization of labor as well as its recoding. While removing territorial boundaries to labor, guest worker programs function to distinguish those human beings labeled "guest worker" from those categorized as citizens, thus recoding what labor requirements have deterritorialized.

Practices associated with illegal immigration are usefully thought of as reterritorializations that take place within the larger context of capitalism's deterritorializations. They are practices of marking territory motivated by the desire for order and unity. They are however, also practices that provide capitalism with the compensatory reterritorializations that Deleuze and Guattari discuss. Kearney suggests that the goal of immigration policy is not in fact to make our borders impermeable but to regulate the flow, to effect the alienation of labor from its owners.[51] Peter Andreas calls attention to the symbolic nature of US border policies, which are more appropriately thought of as an elaborate performance whose goal is to reaffirm the importance of the border and "our" control over it rather than to actually deter illegal crossings.[52] "Deadly Game" is the title of an article in *The Village Voice*, describing the journey of Antonio Gonzalaz from his home town in Zapotitlan de Salinas in southern Mexico to the Bronx, New York where his older brother Juan Carlos paid smugglers $1,600 for Antonio and where he will join the Mexican community in New York where four out of five of the 300,000 come from Puebla.[53] "Game" is becoming an increasingly appropriate metaphor to convey the conflicting desires that lurk beneath US immigration policies. It is a bloody game, though, a deadly one resulting in what Gloria Anzaldua describes as an open wound "where the Third World grates against the first and bleeds. And before a scab forms it hemorrhages again, the lifeblood of two worlds merging."[54]

4   The empire comes home to Britain

Introduction

> In four languages, the signs on the walls in the Red Cross shelter warn of the hazards of trying to sneak into England through the Channel Tunnel: electrocution risk, squashing risk, very high speed train, mortal danger. But even the people who have posted the lists, don't expect them to do much good. Just last week, nine Romanian immigrants including a three year old girl, were found hidden in the undercarriage of a high-speed passenger train that had arrived in London. In near freezing temperatures, they had been traveling at speeds of 180 miles an hour. Passengers heard them banging for help.[1]

Britain is now the most popular destination for immigrants in Europe. A recently released Home Office report estimates that between 150,000 and 175,000 migrants from outside the European Union will enter the country every year until 2005. Many of the entrants are people joining relatives already settled in Britain. Many others are asylum-seekers. However, Britain's need for workers has also fueled the trend.[2] Immigration minister, Barbara Roche points out that Britain is suffering skills shortages in acute areas that go unfilled despite training schemes available to the unemployed.[3] Immigrants are essential for Britain's health, social services, and pension systems. Without net migration over the next twenty-five years, it is predicted that the ratio of people between the ages of 16 and 64 to those over 65 will fall from more than four to fewer than three affecting the ability to maintain these various social services.[4] This need for immigrants occurs amidst an asylum crisis, increases in racist incidents many of which are aimed at immigrants and asylum-seekers,[5] and a redoubling of efforts to "slam shut the floodgates on illegal immigration."[6]

This dilemma is, of course, nothing terribly new for Great Britain, which was one of the first countries to experience the post Second

World War reversals of population movements whereby people from the "Third World" moved to the rich industrialized countries of the West. Docking in London on a cold June morning in 1948, the SS Empire Windrush delivered 500 passengers from Jamaica, black men in suits carrying British passports and hungry for waiting jobs.[7] Symbolically at least, this marked the beginning of the coming home of the Empire to Great Britain. For the first time, large numbers of people who were not white had arrived to live and work among the British at home.[8] The arrival of these Jamaican men coincided with the passage of the 1948 British Nationality Act, which guaranteed the right of all Commonwealth citizens as well as citizens of the United Kingdom and Colonies to enter the United Kingdom without restriction.[9] The "Commonwealth idea" embodied in this legislation was expressive of the desire for a deterritorialized British national identity and helped the British to assuage the "sense of personal loss – almost an amputation" that occurred whenever a part of the empire was granted independence.[10] The anxieties and insecurities brought about by the loss of empire, the simultaneous fall from status as one of the world's major powers, and a severe labor shortage produced in Britain a desire that was both deterritorializing in its erasure of national territorial borders as criterion for citizenship and paranoiac in its subsequent reterritorializing practices that drew heavily on race as a distinguishing marker of who belonged and who did not.[11]

The notion of a deterritorialized Commonwealth identity whereby all subjects of the empire were equal and racial differences were not relevant in terms of citizenship and free movement was put to the test by the non-white composition of immigration from the New Commonwealth countries. Underlying and undermining to the ostensibly universalistic notion of brotherhood and solidarity was a desire for order that manifested itself in the steady move toward ever more restrictive and neo-racist positions on immigration. The "rising tide" of "colored" immigration led to increasing social unease about immigration that continues into the present. Restrictive immigration policies began with the Commonwealth Immigrants Act of 1962 whereby the first controls were placed on immigration from the New Commonwealth, continued with additional acts in 1968 and 1971, and culminated in the British Nationality Act of 1981, which significantly modified the doctrine of *jus soil* (acquisition of nationality by birth) and thus the traditional nature of British citizenship. Two themes that are illustrative of neo-racism and its implication in practices of statecraft became prominent in the debates and discussions on immigration; (1) the issue of social order and fears of disorder and (2) the notion that there exists a kind of threshold, a level of tolerance based on some ill-defined number of immigrants that a society can tolerate before it experiences conflict and social disorder. These themes continue to be prominent in contemporary discussions and policies on asylum. They are by no means unique to Britain and appear in various manifestation in all of the cases examined in this study.

Threshold of tolerance in Britain

> There is no way of understanding English patriotism that averts its eyes from the fact that it has as its centre a feeling for persons of one's own kind.[12]

> We are a British nation with British characteristics. Every nation can take some minorities, and in many ways they add to the richness and variety of this country. But the moment a minority threatens to become a big one, people get frightened.[13]

That outsiders pose a threat to "one's own kind," or one's own race or breed and that this is a natural concern is a hallmark of neo-racism and was clearly evident in the early debates over immigration. Conservative Party member Cyril Osborne was an outspoken proponent of this view in the debates prior to passage of the 1962 Immigration Act. Listen to his words.

> Because of the sheer weight of these numbers something must be done quickly or there will be such tragedies as will frighten most of us. ...Difficult and frightening as are the figures of immigrants from West Indies they pale in significance compared with the figures for the first six months from India and Pakistan. They are really terrifying in their significance.[14]

While no overt mention of race was made the idea prevailed that fewer non-white people made for better race relations. Dramatic phrases that were widely used such as the "sheer weight of numbers," "flood of immigrants," and "tide of immigrants," are assignifying signs that deliver themselves over to the desire for order, unity, and an ultimately unattainable pure identity. The signs themselves are events, symbols of a threat to order and a danger posed by those deemed "other." Surely a signifier such as "the sheer weight of numbers" should have actual numbers as a minimum condition of identity. However, this phrase did not refer in any concrete, objective sense to the number of immigrants entering Britain. It did not, for example, signify white immigrants from Ireland who totaled approximately 60,000–70,000 annually while Commonwealth immigrants totaled only 43,000 in 1955 and 21,000 in 1959.[15]

Ideas of "one's own kind" and dangers associated with too much dilution by outsiders easily shaded into fears that the presence of "others" posed a threat to the British way of life, to the very identity of the British people, as if that identity itself was self-evident and given. In the words of a prominent Catholic publication, "Sure it is not illiberal to be concerned with preserving their own character and continuity. A question which affects the future of our own race and breed is not one that we should leave merely to chance."[16] As noted in Chapter 1, practices of statecraft can come from numerous locales. This desire for the pedagogical, the pure presence of an inside of order and certainty, was most powerfully symbolized in the concept of an "alien wedge" articulated by Enoch Powell in his famous "Rivers of Blood" speech in April 1968 in Birmingham. The movement and flux represented by the "alien wedge" attested to the absence of any precise and unambiguous point of differentiation between the inside realm of the truly British and the ambiguous outside realm of otherness. Desire lurked in this non-place of anxiety doing its productive work constructing, however provisionally, the true British as well as the imposter, the bogus. The "alien wedge" presented a threat to British national identity, culture, and society. Neo-racism was clearly evident in the notion that too much mixing of people with different national characteristics would be harmful and that it was natural to feel this way. Fewer non-white people would make for better race relations. This was apparent not only in calls for severely restricting immigration, but in arguments promoting the dispersal of those immigrants admitted.

> Therefore, I would say that we should be selective in our attitude towards the immigrants whom we take in and to welcome in particular, those who seek dispersal, that is to say those who do not seek or do not wish to live, for social or cultural or religious reasons, in their own community.[17]

> ... social strains tend to develop, as the House knows, where there are large concentrations of coloured people in large towns and cities, as so far as possible coloured immigrants should be enabled to disperse themselves throughout the community instead of congregating together.[18]

The idea of a racial threshold was apparent in demands that local schools restrict the number of Asian and black immigrant children allowed to attend, which resulted in the bussing of immigrant children to schools outside their areas.[19] Even those who were liberals when it came to domestic race relations accepted the argument that harmonious race relations in Britain depended on rapidly cutting down the numbers of non-whites admitted into the country.[20] The Labour Party had been vehemently opposed to the 1962 Immigration Act and had argued against the coded language in which no official reference to race was made but whose absence actually highlighted the glaring presence of race as a criterion for the right of entry. "To use the words we hear so often, 'the social strains and stresses', in simpler and rather cruder language, that phrase really means colour prejudice."[21] Despite their pledge to repeal the Act when and if they took over government, by 1965 the Labour Party fully accepted the Conservative case for controls of non-white immigration and had in fact implemented even greater controls.[22]

The Labour government under Harold Wilson passed The Commonwealth Immigrants Act of 1968 aimed at ending the freedom of entry of Asians with British passports. This emergency legislation was introduced by Home Secretary, James Callaghan. "I regret the need for this bill," he told parliament. "I repudiate emphatically the suggestion that it is racialist in origin or in conception or in the manner in which it is being carried out."[23] Secret cabinet papers recently released suggest that the bill was in fact clearly based on the desire to keep non-white immigrants out of Britain. Six weeks after the bill was passed Callaghan wrote in a memo "It is sometimes argued that we can take a less serious view of the scale of immigration and settlement in this country because it could be, and currently is being, more than offset by total emigration. This view overlooks the important point that emigration is largely by white persons from nearly every corner of the United Kingdom, while immigration and settlement are largely by coloured persons into a relatively small number of concentrated areas."[24] Clearly skin color was a significant issue, but it was inextricably linked with cultural differences that were presumed to be threatening to social order. Callaghan recently told a BBC interviewer "Public opinion in this country was extremely agitated, and the consideration that was in my mind was how we could preserve a proper sense of order in this country and at the same time do justice to these people – I had to balance both considerations."[25] Callaghan's remarks illustrate the significance of the desire for order in practices of statecraft as well as the presumed centrality of racial divisions to the maintenance of that order. With the passage of this act, the right of entry for holders of British passports was removed unless at least one parent or grandparent was born in Britain.

A group of East African Asians filed a complaint against Britain regarding the 1968 Act, with the European Commission on Human Rights in 1970. The Commission, whose report was kept secret for over twenty years, upheld the complaint. Britain increased the annual quota of entry vouchers. When Idi Amin decided to expel British Indians from Uganda in 1972 the 1968 Act proved impossible to enforce and Britain was obliged to accept approximately 30,000 Ugandans.[26] This is illustrative of the constant tension that governments must manage in the construction of the domain of "the inside" and how this is always being negotiated with what is considered "the outside." The newly accepted Ugandan Asians were now, at least in a physical sense, on the inside of Britain. However, reterritorializing practices were at work in the designation of "red zones" and "green zones." Red zones were areas where the size of the Asian population was judged too high and were thereby out of bounds for Ugandan refugees. Green zones were areas where these refugees could be tolerated.[27] Policies of dispersal as well as accompanying designations such as red and green zones might initially seem at odds with strategies of containment and separation. However, I believe it would be a mistake to interpret these as efforts to welcome immigrants into the larger community rather than having them concentrated in particular areas. These policies were motivated by an amorphous and generalized fear of the "other" and the antagonism and disorder that is presumed to result from their presence. This anxiety is what underlies the notion of a "threshold of tolerance." Dispersal policies are not necessarily inconsistent with containment and separation of "strangers" discussed in Chapter 2. This is clearly illustrated in contemporary policies of dispersing asylum-seekers, which is discussed later.

The Immigration Act of 1971 institutionalized the "alien wedge" articulated by Enoch Powell in his 1968 speech. Prior to the 1971 Act, Commonwealth immigrants were not considered "aliens." The construct of "alien" has a long history in Britain going back to the sixteenth century. The 1905 Aliens Act provided for the expulsion of those deemed "undesirable." An Aliens Restriction Act passed during the First World War in 1914 empowered the home secretary to control the registration, movement, and deportation of anyone classified as "alien." A new aliens act was passed in 1919 to extend the 1914 legislation to peacetime. This act allowed the government to deport those who were considered seditious.[28] With passage of the 1971 Act,

Commonwealth immigrants were no longer distinguished from "aliens" and no longer had any privileged right of entry. The desire of statecraft was apparent in the construct of "patrial," which functioned to reterritorialize British citizenship and recode Commonwealth immigrants as laborers. Only those classified as "patrials" were permitted free entry.[29] They were not liable to deportation, could settle and apply for UK passports, were entitled to vote, run for office, and work in nationalized industries.[30] Non-patrials were permitted entry predominantly on the basis of work permits and became subject to control by annual work permits. Their identities were thus officially reduced to the status of laborer. Patrials were also entitled, under the 1972 Treaty of Accession between the United Kingdom and the European Community (later the EU), as UK nationals to freedom of movement within the Community. The vast majority who qualified for the category of patrial were white. Non-patrials were essentially reduced to the category of guest workers and denied the freedom of movement that patrials had.

> The Act was introduced in the belief that there is a limit to which a society can accept large numbers of people from different cultures without unacceptable social tensions. That remains our view.[31]

Immigration policy in Britain is still fundamentally defined by the 1971 Act. The Labour government of 1974–1979, which had opposed the Act did not repeal it or challenge its basic principles. Subsequent legislation and administrative changes have essentially been attempts to improve the system it created. The British Nationality Act of 1981 created an even narrower definition of British citizenship, significantly modifying the doctrine of *jus soil* (acquisition of nationality by birth) and thus the traditional nature of British citizenship. Being born on British soil or in British territorial waters is no longer sufficient to be regarded as British.[32] Racial and cultural differences were again evident and surfaced in the debates prior to passage of this Act. Referring to an amendment offered by Roy Hattersly to re-establish the principle of *jus soil*, Harvey Proctor argued that such an amendment would "extend the rights of British citizenship far wider than it would be wise to do. …The question whether there should be a multi-racial society has never been put before the electorate. If the electorate had ever been offered the opportunity to give an opinion I know what the result would have been. It would not have been in favour of the position in which, unfortunately, we find ourselves, with an immigrant community in our midst ranging from 2.5 million to 3 million."[33] This quote is quite telling. The positions in which "we find ourselves" signifies a differentiation between the "we" who are presumed not to include those who would make Britain a multi-racial society (despite their physical presences) and the immigrants who have forced such a society on the "indigenous white population." Widening the right to citizenship would have a polluting effect on this indigenous element.

Another immigration act was passed in 1988 for the purpose of tightening up various provisions of the 1971 Act. Specifically, it repealed the section of the 1971 Act, which had exempted male Commonwealth citizens settled or born in the United Kingdom from the requirement to provide adequate maintenance for their dependents before they were permitted to enter and restricted the right of entry to just one of the wives of polygamous men. The 1988 Act also severely limited the scope of appeals for those without UK citizenship and constrained the right to appeal against deportation for those seeking refugee status.[34]

Brah suggests that what signals the newness of "neo-racism" is its articulation within the ideological matrix of "nation" and "people." This articulation resonated with a long history of racialized exclusions and enabled the representation of cultures of peoples from the former colonies as not only different but also a threat to the "British way of life."[35] Clearly skin color was significant, if often silent, in these representations. The articulation of race, nation, and people persists as Britain continues to be characterized by the tension between the need for labor and the impossible desire to detach this labor from human beings to whom it is inherently connected. Despite anti-immigrant rhetoric and laws, the number of work permit holders and their dependants has risen by more than a third since Labour came to power with the sharpest increase coming from Africa.[36]

Immigration and criminality

The concern with social order is perhaps most readily apparent in fears of crime and the accompanying concern with law and order. Immigration and race early on became linked with and occupied a central position in the issue of crime creating a contemporary version of a "dangerous class." As far back as the early twentieth century, black seaman who settled in port towns such as Cardiff, Liverpool, and London were constructed in much the same way as the "the pauper" discussed in Chapter 2. They were seen as possessing social values outside the mainstream and a potential threat to the rest of the society.[37] During the late 1950s and early 1960s, the issue of immigration control was intimately tied to the question of black immigrant involvement in criminal activities. This was evident in the debates prior to passage of the 1962 Immigration Act. Listen to the words of Patricia Hornsby-Smith, Joint Under-Secretary of State for the Home Department

> ... certain types of immigrants possess a propensity to live on the immoral earnings of women and to traffic in dangerous drugs.[38]

and Norman Pannel

> For example, colonial and Commonwealth immigrants are responsible for practically the whole of the drug traffic in this country.[39]

The linking of immigration and crime constructed the non-white immigrant as a dangerous element of society, an "enemy within" that was a threat to the order, stability, and identity of the British nation. In such a context the effects of immigration control were no longer limited to geographical border policing. Up until the 1970s, immigration control still basically consisted of restrictions on entry from the external realm with the focus on keeping people out.[40] The linking of immigration and crime constructed non-white immigrants as a dangerous element of society, an "enemy within" that was a threat to the order, stability, and identity of the British nation. The realm of the other, those who did not truly belong was no longer on the territorial outside. The internal other became a concern. Greater domestic controls accompanied restrictive immigration laws. Even before the 1971 Act went into effect a new national police unit concerned with immigration was set up within the Metropolitan Police, the Illegal Immigration Intelligence Unit (IIIU). Its object was to "receive, collate, evaluate, and disseminate information on known or suspected offenders."[41] It was supposed to be informed of searches for illegal entrants, forged identity cards, and passports. It worked closely with the Immigration Services Intelligence Unit and with the Central Drug Intelligence Unit.

The 1971 Immigration Act instituted a system of internal controls. The desire for order was evident in the wide police powers of arrest without warrant in cases of suspected illegal entry, breach of conditions of entry, and harboring illegal entrants.[42] The effect of this was to increase police involvement in the enforcement of immigration control, leading to passport and workplace raids. Changes in 1977 to immigration rules regarding "marriages of convenience" also resulted in expanded police involvement. The police became more involved in the investigation of whether marriages were in fact marriages of convenience.[43] There were cases of Asian women arriving in Britain being subjected to "virginity tests" and of Asian children undergoing X-ray examinations in order to establish their age.[44]

An investigation into the growing tensions between the black community and the police was undertaken by the Select Committee on Race Relations and Immigration during 1971 and 1972. While the media had perceived that a section of the black community was disproportionately involved in criminal activities, the Committee concluded "beyond doubt, colored immigrants are no more involved in crime than others; nor are they generally more concerned in violence, prostitution and drugs."[45] The overall view that emerged from this report was that blacks were either less criminal than whites or similar in their criminal behavior.[46] Gilroy suggests that this view took a radical turn during the years from 1971 to 1976 when a new definition of blacks as a law and order problem emerged.[47] Attention focused on the issue of mugging, which became virtually synonymous with black crime. The politicization and racialization of mugging was part of the larger societal concern with violence and the breakdown in order. The imagery of violence and decay became synonymous with inner city areas where black immigrants had settled.[48] Blacks were constructed as a dangerous class, "that threatening, little-known, and subterranean class so widespread throughout nineteenth century urban society."[49]

Several incidents in the 1970s–1980s reinforced this construction. In August 1976, violence erupted at the annual Carnival in Notting Hill when a major confrontation between young blacks and the police took place. Scotland Yard had sent 1,500 uniformed officers to police the Carnival even before any rioting took place, thus creating a sense of tension. This took on symbolic significance in terms of black crime, disorder, and the police. Following the riots, the pockets of black settlement in which the disorderly minority were thought to live were subjected to a policy of containment. This policy identified certain neighborhoods as high crime areas using statistics for muggings to support this designation. Special squads of anti-mugger police were set up in these areas. The containment policy was significant in that it marked a departure from policing based on the need to combat particular types of crimes toward area-based strategies whereby any inhabitant of a high crime area is apt to be treated as a criminal.[50] Containment functioned as a method of cordoning off from the rest of society those areas where chaos was presumed to reign and order difficult to instill.

Race and criminality were again linked in the representations surrounding the 1981 riots in Brixton in the London borough of Lambeth. Four days prior to the outbreak of riots the police conducted a mass stop and search operation named "Swamp 81." Brixton was flooded with plainclothes officers who stopped over 1,000 people in a period of four days arresting 100. Gilroy has analyzed how these representations constructed blacks as innately criminal and disorder as an expression of black culture.[51] The linking of race and criminality continues. According to recent Home Office figures, black people are more likely than whites to be stopped, searched, and arrested.[52] The Campaign Against Racism and Fascism report that the fear of black crime is still a prominent national theme.[53]

Asylum and intolerance

> It is a racism that is not just directed at those with darker skins, from the former colonial territories, but at the newer categories of the displaced, the dispossessed and the uprooted, who are beating at western Europe's doors, the Europe that helped to displace them in the first place. It is a racism, that is, that cannot be coloured-coded, directed as it is at poor whites as well, and is therefore passed off as xenophobia, a "natural" fear of strangers. But in the way it denigrates and reifies people before segregating and/or expelling them, it is a xenophobia that bears all the marks of the old racism. It is racism in substance, but "xeno" in form.[54]

The idea of a threshold of tolerance continues to be a prominent theme in Britain today, most notably in reference to asylum-seekers. Asylum has in recent years become one of Britain's "hottest political issues." In the year 2000, Britain received the largest number of asylum applicants in Europe.[55] In a fashion similar to the earlier debates on new Commonwealth immigration, the debates on asylum have focused on numbers. Opponents of asylum argue that it is the number of asylum-seekers that gives rise to xenophobia and racism. Integration of asylum-seekers is hindered by the concentration of too many foreigners in any one locality. This view is widely disseminated in the news media.

> Britain is not a racist society, as our long and humane record of accepting genuine refugees proves. Yet it would be irresponsible not to recognize the damage to good race relations threatened by the sheer numbers now arriving.[56]

Neo-racism or what Sivanandan refers to as "xeno-racism" where skin color is not necessarily the predominant source of differentiation is also significant in the asylum issue. This is forcefully illustrated by the events in Dover in recent years. In the autumn of 1997, several hundred asylum-seekers arrived at the port of Dover in Kent. These asylum-seekers were Roma (gypsies) fleeing persecution in Slovakia and the Czech Republic. The charge that they were "bogus" asylum-seekers was echoed in British newspapers, the Tory Kent County Council, Dover's Labour Member of Parliament, Gwyn Prosser, the Labour leader of the local council, Terry Birkett, and the Labour government's Home Office Minister Mike O'Brien. In October, members of the National Front came to Dover distributing "invasion alert" leaflets. In November about fifteen members of the British National Party arrived carrying baseball bats and distributing leaflets proclaiming "Crisis in Dover" in the Folkestone Road area where many of the asylum-seekers were accommodated.[57] When approximately forty members of both the National Front and the British National Party attempted to march along the seafront about 200 anti-fascists showed up and forced them to abandon their march. National Front marches and anti-fascist demonstrations continued into 1998. During the summer and autumn of 1998, refugees fleeing the conflict in Kosovo began arriving in Dover, increasing the number of asylum-seekers to around 400. The next few months witnessed news articles and editorials attacking asylum-seekers, marches, and anti-fascist counter-demonstrations. The events of 1998/1999 in Dover became symbols of the anti-asylum sentiment that spread beyond coastal communities.[58]

The concern with the threat posed by concentrations of asylum-seekers resulted in a controversial dispersal policy, which was instituted in April 2000.[59] The Asylum and Immigration Bill passed in 1999 by a Labour government introduced a policy of forced dispersal of asylum-seekers. This policy institutionalized a practice already being followed by many London boroughs of dispersing asylum-seekers to southern coastal towns and to the north. The Bill expressly prohibited the asylum-seeker's preference from being taken into account in allocating accommodation or location. Areas with unfilled housing were designated "reception zones" and local authorities were obliged to notify the Home Office of all their empty properties. To ensure that asylum-seekers stayed where they were assigned and did not have guests, powers of entry and search of their accommodation were built into the Bill. The Post Office was required to notify the Home Office of any redirection of an asylum-seeker's mail.[60] The result of the dispersal policy has been increased racism and xenophobia in areas where asylum-seekers have been dispersed to. The issue of asylum-seekers dominated political debates in local elections in 152 English councils in May 2000 and reached such a pitch that the United National High Commissioner for Refugees condemned the xenophobic tone of the debate. Xenophobia and racial violence was used by the Labour Party to justify its dispersal policy.[61]

Recently, then Home Secretary, Jack Straw, proposed several plans to deal with immigrants and asylum-seekers. On February 6, 2001, Straw suggested drawing up a list of countries and groups from which asylum applications would be ruled inadmissable. "An EU or internationally agreed list of safe countries or groups from which asylum applications would be ruled inadmissible or considered under a greatly accelerated process ought to be on the agenda."[62] In April 2001, Straw vowed to increase the number of asylum-seekers who are removed from the United Kingdom each year after being refused refugee status. The target for 2001 was 30,000.[63] In May, 2001 immigration officers were given permission by the Home Office to target certain groups at immigration control. The targeted list covers most of the ethnic groups now claiming asylum in the largest numbers; Tamils, Kurds, Albanians, Somalis, Afghans, Roma, Pontic Greeks, and ethnic Chinese. The decision resulted from an extension of race relations laws to cover immigration officials and which required all incoming passengers to be treated equally at passport control. A Home Office spokeswoman said, "It was recognised that it was necessary to discriminate on the grounds of nationality or ethnic origin. The alternative is to subject all passengers of every nationality to the same degree of examination at immigration control, which would lead to significant delays and inconvenience."[64] In July of 2001, the British and Czech governments agreed to allow UK immigration officers to turn away selected travelers in Prague to reduce the number of Czechs seeking asylum in Britain. Most of the Czechs seeking asylum are gypsies. The Czech government agreed to this rather than face a universal visa requirement. The agreement was publicly denounced by politicians and human rights groups as racist when a Roma journalist destined for the same address as his white colleague was turned back by British immigration officers at Prague airport.[65]

The criminality theme also persists in the asylum issue. Straw came under fire for ordering the creation of 500 new places in prisons to house asylum-seekers. The Campaign Against Racism and Fascism reports that the asylum-seekers will be housed in separate wings from the general prison population, but will be subject to the same prison rules and face prison officers who are trained to contain convicted criminals.[66] Britain is currently holding 1,800 detainees, more than 1,000 of them in regular prisons. The United Kingdom has been condemned by the United Nations as the only country in Europe to detain asylum-seekers in prison.[67]

Conclusion

Roy Hattersly writes of listening to a radio program in which Michael Wills MP said that the prime minister had given him the special task of encouraging other members of the government to "pay special respect to our national identity – always in their speeches and whenever possible in their policy decision."[68] Hattersly points out that in order to do this, a working definition of the appropriate national identity will have to be provided. He goes on to suggest that all the easy answers to questions of a national identity have more to do with fascism than philosophy. Arguably, this is an inherent danger of any assertion of a national identity. A recent report on the "Future of Multi-Ethnic Britain" points to the problem of Britain's self identity. "…Britishness, as much as Englishness, has systematic largely unspoken, racial connotations. Whiteness nowhere features as an explicit condition of being British, but it is widely understood that Englishness, and therefore by extension Britishness is racially coded."[69] Such codifications are responses to the tensions created between the desire for order, for a unified and unproblematic identity for Britain and the flow of human beings initiated first by the need for deterritorialized labor and later by the movement of refugees. Immigration policies, nationality laws, and asylum policies were/are performative practices that draw their power from the pedagogical nation. They are invested with a desire for an unambiguous inside of the British nation. These policies are, however, continually producing anew what constitutes the inside of the British nation.

5 Seuil de tolerance[1]

Introduction

> France is becoming, for the first time in its history, and against its will, a true terre d'immigration for peoples of all races. However distressing many French find this transformation, and whatever problems and discomfort all parties are suffering along the way, a confluence of demographic and economic factors on both sides of the Mediterranean ensures that it will continue, as certainly as the disparities between the First and Third Worlds will increase and multiply.[2]

> France cannot live without its own identity.[3]

France, like Britain and the United States, has oscillated between the schizophrenic pole of desire that tends in the direction of infinite freedom, defying boundaries, promoting perpetual flow of goods, capital, and human bodies and the desire for order, for a secure and unproblematic identity that clearly knows the boundaries between what it is and what it is not. The two poles of desire were evident in post Second World War disagreements over whether France should promote mass permanent immigration or whether immigration should be linked to specific areas of employment and to a restrictive concept of a cohesive nation-state. The *laissez faire* approach to immigration that characterized French immigration policy in the immediate post Second World War period is illustrative of the schizophrenic pole, supporting the relatively free and often clandestine movement of foreign workers into France. However, as immigration increased rapidly from the mid-1950s to the late 1960s and as the source of the immigrants became more diverse the second pole of desire became more and more evident. Concerns were raised about the assimilability of the immigrants and what their presence meant for French society. Anxiety was evident regarding the number of immigrants France could tolerate and it became widely accepted as truth that there was in fact a limit to the number of immigrants that could be tolerated. This issue continues to be salient in France. Immigration is increasingly vital to the economy. According to a UN Population Division report France will need to import 1.8 million laborers a year until the year 2050 just to maintain its current ratio of active to retired citizens. At the same time opinion polls show consistently that a majority of French think there are too many foreigners in the country.[4]

Schizophrenic desire, *laissez faire*, and immigrant labor

Laissez faire approaches to immigration uphold the "commodity fiction" that labor can be separated from the human beings to whom it is attached. Human beings are decoded and recoded in terms of their labor power, becoming deterritorialized commodities. Such an approach characterized immigration policy in France in the immediate post Second World War period, who like Britain and other European countries was in need of foreign labor. Despite disagreements over permanent versus temporary immigration, there existed a broad consensus among France's demographers, economists, and politicians that the reconstruction of France would necessitate a substantial increase in foreign labor. Charles de Gaulle argued that the status of France as a great power depended on an increase in population that would require an active immigration policy.[5] That active immigration policy became one that was largely unregulated. Despite the 1945 creation of the National Immigration Office (ONI), which was to have sole responsibility for the recruitment of foreign labor and a series of bilateral agreements with labor exporting countries, foreign labor recruitment was mainly carried out by private employers, was largely spontaneous, and often clandestine.[6] The French government turned a blind eye to the situation and even encouraged it, sometimes tacitly, sometimes openly. In 1966, Minister of Social Affairs, Jean-Marcel Jeanneney, said "Illegal immigration itself is not without a certain value, for were we to pursue a policy of strict enforcement of the rules and international agreements governing this area, we would perhaps lack the manpower we need."[7] A process of regularization enabled immigrants who had arrived illegally or overstayed tourist visas, but had subsequently found work to receive working papers from the government. This process of regularization reached its peak in 1968 when only 18 percent of immigrant workers entered through official channels.[8]

During this period of time the stress was on immigrants as a source of cheap and mobile foreign labor, the market mechanism being the major determinant of their fate. Immigrants were considered a peripheral presence in French society. Reprehensible social conditions developed as immigrants were socially and geographically confined to areas on the outskirts of major cities in slums, which became known as "bidonvilles." (shanty-towns). As Polanyi points out, the human beings who embody labor power would perish without the various protections afforded by social institutions.[9] As human beings perish from the effects of social exposure, the social order itself is threatened. This was precisely the situation as immigrant workers were relegated to the periphery of French society. The marginalization of a significant number of human beings physically within a society problemetizes the very definition of that society. The presence of increasing numbers of human beings in France who were relegated to the margins and were not considered truly part of French society contributed to the tension out of which French society constituted itself. The desire for order motivated practices, which attempted to balance the tensions created by the deterritorialized flows of humanity and the social protection necessary to prevent the destruction of society itself. In the process the boundaries between the inside of French identity and the outside were made problematic.

The concept of governmentality captures the tension between the construction of immigrant labor as an economic commodity and the inherently social human beings in which this labor is embodied. Recall, that according to Foucault, the feat of government broadly defined is to manage the tensions between the non-totalizable multiplicity of economic interests and the noneconomic interests whereby individuals espouse the well-being of the family, the clan, the nation thereby constructing the complex realm of governmentality. Practices of governmentality must continually negotiate and define or redefine the space of the population in order to balance the tensions between the pole of social order and the pole of deterritorialized flows. These practices construct the inside of the nation-state and the subject deemed to "belong." This construction, like the desire that motivates it is not stable and fixed, but always in process, always subject to disruption, always moved by the forces of desire. In response to the deteriorating social conditions several tentative steps were taken in the social realm. In 1966, the Social Action Fund (FAS), an organization created in 1958 for the purpose of addressing the issues of housing, job training, language education, and other social issues for Algerians in France, was expanded in scope to include the welfare of all foreign workers, gypsies, and other minorities.[10] A national commission was also established in 1966 for the purpose of dealing with immigrant housing. These responses, in effect, extended the realm of governmentality incorporating immigrants into the space of the French population.

After 1974, the government become increasingly involved in social efforts pertaining to immigrants, particularly in the areas of housing and welfare services.[11] Antoine Postel-Vinay was appointed Minister of State for Immigrant Workers. He immediately proposed an end to further labor recruitment, coupled with an ambitious program designed to improve the living conditions of immigrants already in France.[12] In 1980, new measures were introduced to improve the housing, employment, and educational prospects of immigrants. Foreign groups were allowed the free right of association, which had previously required the approval of the Interior Ministry. Substantial state funding was made available to support these groups.[13] In July of 1984, the left passed a law granting automatically renewable ten-year combined work and residence permits to the majority of foreigners legally in France. This law was at least partially in response to the demands of immigrant associations who had been pressing for changes in the previous system under which immigrants had to be holders of both a residence and a work permit each of which was valid for one, three, or ten years. The residence and work permits did not necessarily have the same duration, making it difficult to meet this criteria.[14]

The non-European population became increasingly stable in the sense that they became a permanent aspect of French society thus redefining "the population," expanding the realm of governmentality, and thereby reconstructing French society. The effect of the increase in the number of non-Europeans coming into France and the conditions, which resulted from their subsequent marginalization was to add a new dimension to the French discourse on immigration. Immigration was no longer defined as primarily an economic issue, but came to be considered a social problem. Failing to address the issues of concern and consequence to the immigrant community would have rendered them outside the realm of governmentality and thus an uncontrollable "social danger." The focus on integration and assimilation, which is discussed below is consistent with the notion of governmentality.

All of this is not to suggest that non-European immigrants were a welcome addition to French society or that social programs were necessarily inclusive and benign or to suggest that immigrants are not still in many ways considered a social danger to French society. It is merely to illustrate that the definition of French society, the differentiation between the inside and the outside was and is not fixed and static. The assertion of a unified and unproblematic French identity was never a fully mastered accomplishment. It is always subject to slippage and displacement. As noted in Chapter 2, statecraft takes place in the pedagogical and performative double time Homi Bhabha has articulated.[15] The pedagogical is illustrated in France's desire for the self-evident presence of a unified French identity. The performative comes to the fore in policies such as regularization and social welfare, which clearly show the negotiation with flows and flux, which thereby problemetizes but never fully destroys the pedagogical. In this double time the very notion of what it means to be French is redefined.

Neo-racism and the *seuil de tolerance*

As immigration came to be perceived as a social problem and immigrants themselves a danger to the social order, a kind of master theme developed, which came to underpin much of the discourse on immigration. *"Seuil de tolerance"* suggests that there exists a threshold of tolerance in any society concerning the presence of foreigners, beyond which social conflict is inevitable. It grew out of theories of social scientists, but became a working assumption of French policy makers and a large sector of the general public.[16] The "truth" of *seuil de tolerance* came to be widely accepted. At the heart of the idea of *seuil de tolerance* lie the rather slippery concepts of cultures and civilizations to which foreigners and non-foreigners are presumed to belong and is, of course, a variant on the clash of civilizations thesis so in vogue today. Talk of cultures and civilizations easily slide into the equally slippery but powerful concepts of ethnicity and race, which is what occurred in France. The immigration issue was racialized and policies became increasingly restrictive. The shift toward more restrictive immigration policies coincided with the industrial strikes and squatter's agitation in slums and working-class areas in May 1968. Many foreign workers took part in the wave of protests that swept France in May–June 1968 and many were subsequently deported.[17] On July 9, 1968, a circular was issued from the Ministry of Social Affairs, which spelled out new requirements for immigrants. Regularization of manual and semiskilled workers would be prohibited. Resident permits could be refused an immigrant if the job sought was on the list of positions for which there was already an overabundance of workers.

On February 26, 1969, a report defining a new immigration policy for France was presented to and adopted by the Social and Economic

Council. The report, issued by M. Corentin Calvez, detailed the argument that led to the adoption of ethnically selective immigration and that has become the basis for contemporary French immigration policy.[18] The report suggested that the nature of immigration had changed with Europeans being replaced by non-Europeans, especially North Africans. According to the report this fact was disturbing because the non-Europeans were not easily assimilable. The report predicted that by the year 2000 the number of Algerians in France would constitute an "inassimilable island" and therefore it was desirable to "give to the influx of non-European origin, and particularly to the current from the Maghreb, the character of a temporary immigration for work."[19]

Recall that the key defining feature of neo-racism is the notion that bounded communities founded on cultural differences are the natural result of human nature. *Seuil de tolerance* exemplifies this idea. The 1969 report argued that limiting non-Europeans to the status of temporary immigrants and limiting the number of family members of non-Europeans permitted to join their relatives did not constitute discrimination, but rather was motivated by a "profoundly humane preoccupation." As discussed in Chapter 2, neo-racism enables its proponents to turn ideas of racism and intolerance on their heads thereby justifying discriminatory polices on the basis of a respect for difference and a concern with peace and security for all. This is nicely illustrated in the following quotes. In 1970, Michel Massenet, an ardent proponent of *seuil de tolerance* who held a variety of governmental posts dealing with immigration, and was the most influential civil servant in the immigration field suggested that

> In primary school class, the presence of more than 20 per cent of foreign children slows down the progress of all children. In a hospital, problems of coexistence arise when foreigners represent more than 30 per cent of the number of patients. In a block of flats, it is not wise to go beyond the proportion of 10 to 15 per cent of families of foreign origin when these families are not accustomed to life in a modern environment.[20]

In 1981, Charles Hernu, Mayor of Villeurbanne in Lyons, asserted that

> I am striving to disperse them (the immigrants) throughout the city in such a way that no neighborhood surpasses a threshold of ten per cent. I believe that there is a threshold that we cannot exceed without tragedy.[21]

In December 1989, then French President Francois Mitterand declared on national television that the threshold for the numbers of immigrants in France had been reached in the 1970s.[22] In January 1990, Raymond Barre, former Prime Minister under Giscard d'Estaing, suggested that a coherent immigration policy would avoid "large concentrations of immigrants in certain quarters or certain towns."[23] In 1991, leader of the mainstream right party, Rassemblement pour la Republique (RPR), former Prime Minister, and current President, Jacques Chirac suggested,

> we risk exceeding the threshold of tolerance, whose existence has been recognized by the President. It is not sensible to deny it in the name of some anti-racist ideology or other … . We must have an immediate moratorium on family immigration.[24]

The ideas behind a "threshold of tolerance" were thus shared across a wide spectrum of society permitting and justifying exclusionary policies on the grounds of the inevitability of conflict if human beings of different cultures are mixed in inappropriate numbers. Social problems that arose within the context of immigration and the mixing of cultures could be attributed to this "natural law" of human populations. In turn the very existence of those social problems could then be used as evidence to support the "truth" of *seuil de tolerance*.

Intolerance arguably reaches its peak with attempts at deportation, which is a logical though extreme outcome of the belief in a threshold of tolerance. Forcing immigrants deemed culturally different and therefore a threat, to leave re-establishes the pure, authentic social order. From 1977, the discourse on immigration focused on the immigrant as antithetical to the interests of the nation-state. In 1977, Lionel Stoleru, Minister of State for Immigrant Workers, introduced a repatriation scheme which offered 10,000 francs as encouragement to immigrants to return to their countries of origin. The aim was to remove 1 million foreigners from French soil in five years. It failed in that only 57,953 took up the offer and most of these were Spanish and Portuguese workers not the expected non-Europeans. In 1979, President Giscard d'Estaing attempted to repatriate by force 500,000 Algerians, but failed due to widespread opposition by left wing parties, labor unions, and churches as well as the Guallist and Christian-Democratic right wing parties. Interior Minister, Christian Bonnet, proposed a measure under which immigrant workers and their families could be forcibly repatriated if they were deemed to be surplus to current labor requirements.

The measure failed to gain the necessary parliamentary majority, but Bonnet used his discretionary powers to expel on average 5,000 immigrant workers a year between 1978 and 1981 most of whom were young Maghrebis.[25] Under the Bonnet Law of 1980, the expulsion of "irregulars" was made an administrative rather than judicial matter, thus speeding up the process and removing it from the jurisdiction of the law.[26] When the left came to power in 1981, most of the expulsions were stopped and a general amnesty was declared for illegal immigrants provided they had entered France prior to January 1.

Seuil de tolerance is not simply an idea, which justifies exclusionary policies. Freeman points out that while the acceptance of a threshold of tolerance may at first seem to be at odds with the traditional French view of its endless absorbative capacity, these two ostensibly opposed ideas are in fact quite compatible. Only a fully assimilated minority would not activate the process of rejection, the conflicts that mixing different cultures would cause. Assimilation was a key aspect of post Second World War French immigration but was always inextricably linked to the issue of control and exclusion. Rhetoric and policy on assimilation created a dichotomy between the easy absorption of previous European immigrants and the inassimilability of the new (mostly African) immigrants. It thus simultaneously promoted inclusion and exclusion as well as racializing the immigration issue in the process. Ostensibly assimilation implies that those who are assimilated are no longer strangers, no longer "the other." However, the very notion of assimilation presumes the visibility of differences that must be eradicated. It presumes and reaffirms the idea of a homogeneous national collectivity that serves as the exemplar, the superior to which others must strive to assimilate. This is clearly illustrated in the 1994 remarks of Jean-Claude Barreau, adviser on immigration to the French minister of the interior,

> ... when somebody emigrates, he changes not only his country, but also his history. Foreigners arriving to settle in France must understand that from henceforth their ancestors are the Gauls and that they have a new homeland ... . But Muslim extremists have begun arriving in France as colonizers, with gods and weapons in their baggage. ...Today, there is a real Islamic threat in France which is part of a great worldwide wave of Muslim fundamentalism.[27]

The project of assimilation is a manifestation of the desire for an authentic core, which would identify the true and pure nationals.

Insofar as such an authentic core cannot be found (and arguably does not exist) assimilation becomes a quest for an inaccessible goal, but it also becomes a process by which the true and the false, the good and the bad, those who belong and those who do not are constructed. Despite its ostensibly inclusionary character, assimilation can work to differentiate, externalize, and construct "the other" in terms of dangers and threats. The discourse of assimilation and control constructed the Third World immigrant as a stranger, albeit a stranger whose presence was long term or even permanent. The physical closeness, yet social and political remoteness of the immigrants problemtized the notion of France as a unitary society with a shared sense of national identity. Policies of assimilation aimed to recode the immigrants as French and thereby reterritorialize their identity within French society. There was always a slippage though between those who were "genuinely" French and the promises of assimilation. As Balibar notes,

> No theoretical discourse on the dignity of all cultures will really compensate for the fact that, for a 'Black' in Britain or a 'Beur' in France, the assimilation demanded of them before they can become 'integrated' into the society in which they already live (and which will always be suspected of being superficial, imperfect, or simulated) is presented as progress, as an emancipation, a conceding of rights.[28]

Pasqua, paranoiac desire, and the *Sans Papier*

Immigration figured prominently in the 1986 general election, which was a victory for the mainstream right, with the National Front (FN) gaining its first parliamentary seat.[29] The Pasqua approach to immigration, named after Interior Minister Charles Pasqua advocated a policy of winning FN votes by pursuing tough immigration policies championed by FN leader, Jean Marie Le Pen. This approach was followed between 1986 and 1988 and then again in 1993. The Pasqua Laws are symbols of severe anti-immigrant measures, emblematic of the desire for order, to once and for all purge the realm of disorder and impurities. The Pasqua Law and the subsequent Debre Law, discussed below, led to opposition on the part of the Catholic Church, human rights groups, academics, and the United Nations.

The 1986 legislation gave the executive control over deportations on the grounds of protecting public order. This legislation widened the categories of those liable to be expelled and made access to the ten-year residence and work permits discussed above subject to restrictions.

One of the first deportations under the new legislation was a mass deportation of 101 Malians, chained together in a specially chartered aircraft. Within a year after the 1986 Pasqua Law came into force there were 17,000 deportations.[30] The 1993 legislation limited the rights of asylum-seekers, facilitated easier identity checks by police, limited entry and residence rights of foreigners, and amended Article 23 of the Code de la Nationalite Francaise (French Nationality Code) abandoning *droit du sol*, the principle of granting citizenship to all those born on French soil. Article 23 originally conferred French Nationality automatically on anyone born in France having at least one parent who was also born on French territory. Under this article, the children of Algerian immigrants as well as certain other former colonies were automatically citizens because these areas had been French territories. The 1993 legislation amended Article 23 so that citizenship was not automatic. After January 1, 1994, children born in France of immigrant parents had to apply for French citizenship between the ages of 16 and 21. Parents could not apply for citizenship for their under-age children. Children born in France to Algerian parents would be French from birth only if one of their parents had lived in France for at least five years prior to their birth.[31] Under the Pasqua approach public surveillance was intensified. Officials in public services such as the post office, hospitals, social insurance, tax, and labor offices were ordered to check clients' papers and report "irregulars" to the authorities. "Supporting illegal residence" was punishable by imprisonment or a fine. The Pasqua Laws were widely criticized by supporters of immigrants' rights. Maurice Glele-Ahanhanzo, a human right's expert from Benin and Special Rapporteur of the UN Commission on Human Rights suggested that "France is being shaken by a wave of xenophobia and racism that is highly prejudicial to its image as the homeland of human rights."[32]

The Pasqua Laws contained an interesting gap, which ironically problemetized the very classification scheme it ostensibly sought to reinforce, that is, the binary opposition between legal immigrants with the right to stay and the duty to assimilate and illegal immigrants who should be made to leave. This gap stemmed from the fact that the requirement for children born in France with immigrant parents, to apply for citizenship at age 18 was not retroactive. Under the 1993 laws, undocumented parents of children who were French citizens could not legally be expelled, but were prevented from receiving residence papers. This created the category of the *Sans Papiers* (the paperless, without papers) who could not be deported, but could not be legalized either. This category eventually came to refer to the broader group of immigrants who, for various reasons, were without papers.

The issue of the *Sans Papiers* received widespread attention in 1996 when a group of immigrants (some 230 in number) from Africa (mostly Mali) consisting of men, women, and children occupied Saint Bernard Church near Montmartre in Paris.[33] For a variety of reasons the immigrants were all without valid papers. Some had had their application for asylum rejected. Some were the spouses of legal immigrants but were not entitled to live in France. Some were visa overstayers, or persons born in France of foreign parents. The immigrants began their occupation in June and stayed in the church for two months. Many of the protesters went on a hunger strike, demanding one-year work permits, which the government denied. The immigrants appointed a "college of mediators," which was composed of eminent French academics, jurists, ecclesiastics, and human rights activists to negotiate their position. On August 12, police entered the church to remove ten hunger strikers. They were taken to a nearby hospital for check-ups and most returned to the church the same day. The Interior Minister examined the files of the immigrants and granted visas to twenty-two of them. On August 23, weeks after negotiations between the mediators and the Chirac administration had broken down, French security forces raided Saint Bernard, sweeping aside protesters who supported the *Sans Papiers*, breaking down the church doors, and evacuating the immigrants. They removed ninety-eight men, fifty-four women, and sixty-eight children from the church. The next day, some were flown home, others freed by court order, and others ordered to leave by September 12. Subsequent hearings revealed that the police had separated people inside the church by skin color, inadvertently taking into custody a number of black French nationals. Other procedural violations had occurred such as isolation of the detainees from counsel. Many of the immigrants were released because of such violations.[34]

In the Fall of 1996, Minister of the Interior, Jean-Louis Debre introduced a bill in the same spirit and following the same logic of the Pasqua Laws. The bill called on the government to keep files on anyone who housed foreigners and empowered the government to confiscate the passports of asylum-seekers and foreigners whose situation is judged "irregular." This enabled prefects (regional representatives of the central authorities) to expel foreigners, something only the minister of the interior could previously do. The bill also made it easier for foreigners with a French spouse or French children to obtain residence permits.[35] In February 1997, the French National Assembly approved this new immigration legislation by a large margin. The law was aimed at illegal immigrants from former French colonies in Africa and North Africa. Europeans and visitors from about thirty other countries were exempt from the reporting requirement. The bill, as passed, created a national registry of French citizens and their foreign guests. It permitted officials to take the fingerprints of anyone from outside the European Union applying for a residence permit.[36] One provision of the new legislation required foreigners without residency permits who stayed in private homes to report their arrival and departure to the local police.[37] Other provisions of the new law required permanent resident foreigners to prove that they were not "a threat to public order." Police were permitted to search workplaces for illegal employees as well as immigrants' vehicles, and confiscate the passports of foreigners lacking required residency papers.[38] The law resulted in protests on the part of immigrant supporters. On February 27, the European Parliament passed a resolution urging the French government to withdraw the immigration bill. President Chirac denounced the Parliament for interfering in France's internal affairs.[39] On March 26, 1997, this new immigration law, the Debre Law, named after Interior Minister Debre was approved by the French Parliament.

The *Sans Papier* had gained public support and in February 1997, 100,000 people in Paris demonstrated against Debre. The left wing who won elections in June 1997, had campaigned, in part, on immigration reform. "Nothing is more alien to France than xenophobia and racism," said the new Socialist Prime Minister, Lionel Jospin.[40] The Chevenement Law had been announced during the campaign as a radical change in governmental logic regarding immigration that would replace the Pasqua Laws. The new laws were named after the new Minister of the Interior, Jean-Pierre Chevenement, and were based on a report by a commission headed by political scientist Patrick Weil.[41] On April 8, 1998, the National Assembly gave final approval to the new law. It modified, but did not repeal the Pasqua and Debre Laws. The vote split the ruling left-wing coalition, with the Socialists voting in favor of it and the Communists and Greens against it or abstaining. Under the new law, children born in France to foreign parents become French citizens automatically provided the child has lived in France for at least five years after his or her eleventh birthday.[42]

In June of 1998, France granted amnesty to 70,000 of the 150,000 immigrants considered *"Sans Papier"* because of their lack of papers. This left 80,000 to be removed. Many of these immigrants facing deportation occupied the Vatican embassy in Paris the first weekend in August 1998, but left after the French interior minister said their cases would be reconsidered and the embassy asked them to leave.[43] The issue of the *Sans Papier* highlights the contradictory nature of statecraft in the era of globalization. Supporters problematize the idea of geographical borders, and national identities as the criteria for belonging and all that belonging entails. Opponents raise the specter of fear of the nomad, of strangers on the "inside." The practices surrounding this issue illustrate the complex nature of governmentality, the perpetual definition and redefinition of who is within the realm of French "society."

The shadow of anti-immigrantism

Immigration continues to be a contentious and emotionally charged issue in France as it does in the United States, Britain, and elsewhere. This is clearly illustrated in the recent events in France in which Le Pen won 17 percent of the vote in the first round presidential elections on April 21, 2002. Le Pen had promised to deport illegal migrants, defend poor white families in housing developments around Paris, and give preference to native French in jobs and welfare. This policy of "national preference" under which social security benefits, housing, and employment would be available to "native French" before anyone else is a euphemism for legal discrimination against immigrants. It is illustrative of the slippage between the "genuine" and those who must be assimilated, those who as Balibar pointed out will always be suspected of being superficial and imperfect.[44] In 1998, former Prime Minister, Edouard Balladur of the RPR, had called for a special commission to consider the FN's policy of "national preference." Any such policy, is of course, another way of constructing the true and authentic from the "others" and functions to create an "outside" within that could potentially be excluded from social protection policies. Commenting on his policy of national preference, Le Pen said

> The United Nations says that Europe needs 29 million immigrants to keep the economy going. I would rather eat dry bread and do without immigrants.[45]

Le Pen received the most votes in neighborhoods near concentrations of immigrants, including 23 percent of the vote in Marseilles, Frances second largest city.[46] "Foreigners arrive, get houses and welfare benefits and do nothing."[47] After splitting in December 1998, the FN has more recently gained wider support as illustrated in the 2002 elections.[48] While there are numerous reasons for this, concerns over law and order and the immigration issues remain central

> We need to make sure that more goes to the French and less to the foreigners.[49]

While French voters did not elect Le Pen, it has been suggested that the "fuel for future anti-immigrant and anti-Europe politicians remains among voters worried by crime, immigrants, European integration, and economic globalization."[50] In May, the French state railway company announced that it would spend $6.6 million dollars on extra security measures to keep migrants away from the Channel tunnel between France and Britain. These measures include a double-barbed wire fence around the perimeter of the Frethun yard and an infra-red detector. In June, France agreed to draw up a timetable for the closure of the Red Cross Sangatte refugee camp. The camp, which was built in 1999 near Calais, has been a constant source of tension between France and Britain. The camp is a half a mile from the Channel Tunnel and it has been estimated that some 200 refugees a night attempt to cross through the tunnel by various means.[51]

Conclusion

Bauman suggests that order is continuously engaged in a war of survival, which entails efforts to exterminate ambivalence, to define precisely and to suppress or eliminate everything that cannot be precisely defined. "Life seems more and more precarious even in Gisors, where we live comfortably. So people like the sound of someone who says they can shut all the problems out" says the plumber quoted above. The construction of order, however sets the limits to incorporation and admission. As Bauman notes, securing supremacy for a designed, artificial order is a two-pronged task. It demands the unity and integrity of the internal realm and the security of the borders separating it from the external realm. Both sides of the task converge in one effort, that of separating the inside from the outside, making the boundary of the organic structure sharp and clearly marked. Attempts to do this in post Second World War France illustrate the usefulness of the understanding of "the state" suggested in Chapter 1. Immigration related policies were characterized by a process, which simultaneously coded and recoded the identity of those human beings who were to be considered "authenitically" French, thus to reaffirm the unity of the internal realm. However, this very process redefined what "authentically" French was in fact and thus reterritorialized the internal realm. The inherent instability of this realm was thereby exposed. The desire for purity, for the unambiguous differentation from the external realm is the ideal that is "the state." Its concrete manifestation took place within a context traversed by the initial need for foreign labor and the previously constructed ideals of universality and assimilation. Statecraft oscillated between the desire for order and stability and the facilitation of flows of human beings. While France proclaims a "zero option" policy on immigration and has authorized no new immigration since 1974, the facts suggest a more complicated story. One study predicts that from 16 to 20 million additional young immigrants will settle in France by the year 2050.[52] The desire for purity continues as well. A 1997 poll conducted by Le Monde found that 60 percent of respondents said there were too many Arabs in France. A March, 2000 Harris opinion poll reported that 63 percent said there were too many Arabs and 38 percent said there were too many blacks.[53] An informal survey by a reporter for the *San Francisco Chronicle* observed forty-five young men and women who were visibly Arab or black being stopped and asked for their papers in a two-hour period at the Gare du Nord railway station in metropolitan Paris.[54]

Neo-racism has been an integral aspect of this desire for a pure unambiguous space of national identity, a space, which was (and continues to be) widely perceived as threatened by the flow of deterritorialized human bodies. This is not to suggest a functionalist understanding of racism. The ways in which "race" becomes articulated into the immigration issue calls for a flexible and nuanced conceptualization of "race." Silverman and others have suggested racisms as opposed to one universal and timeless racism, permitting the concept to have relative mobility and flexibility, which can articulate with various discourses in a variety of diverse times and places.[55] Neo-racism is one of the racisms that functions within the context of contemporary globalization and immigration, and has been a significant aspect of contemporary practices of statecraft.

6 In closing and reflection

They're not ignorant of the range of intellectual, artistic, culinary and commercial influences that have enriched their countries, particularly their cities. But for the most part they can't get over the fear that immigrants dilute their local and national cultures.[1]

Across Europe the forces of reaction and intolerance are on the march. It would be extraordinarily complacent to believe that it could not happen in this country too.[2]

Fear, anxiety, insecurity, the perpetual echoing of that soft, but persistent voice whispering "our walls are made of plastic, our acropolis of paper-mache."[3] Today this voice resounds throughout the rich, industrialized countries of the Western world as the boundaries that separate rich and poor become increasingly traversed by the numerous elements of globalization. And nothing seems to elicit such intense anxiety more than the human beings who pin their hopes and dreams and lives on the crossing of dangerous borders. The Southern Poverty Law Center in the United States reports a recent upswing in anti-immigrant activism as well as growing transnationalism among extremist groups.[4] In May, 2002, Denmark adopted Europe's toughest immigration laws. Across Europe, there are calls for the European Union to create a common border guard and crack down on illegal migrants.[5] It is surely ironic that as geographic spaces of the West (e.g. the deserts of the southwestern United States, the beaches of southern Spain, the chunnel between France and Britain) become deathtraps for Africans, Mexicans, Guatemalans, Chinese, and many "others" on the down side of life and globalization, it is in the countries whose governments build the fences, install the razor wire, and board the refugee ships with machine guns and automatic weapons that insecurity lurks so very near to the surface.[6]

This insecurity and the accompanying desire for order seems to have reached a new level of intensity recently, due in part but not solely to the events of September 11. Hardly a day goes by that one cannot read a headline attesting to the potential dangers of immigration or the renewed efforts to keep "them" out, or the failed attempts to keep "them" out, or the "successful" border policies that have in fact kept "them" out only to result in many, many deaths as "they" continually try to get in. In an article entitled "Europe's Unwelcome Guests," *The Nation*, proclaims that resentment against immigrants is at the boil.[7] *The Guardian* states that "Pim is dead but his ideas are more alive than ever."[8] *The New York Times* speaks of "Europe's Identity Crisis."[9] A common element in the rightward move in Europe recently is the issue of immigration and the fears it raises and while September 11 may have exacerbated these fears, they were present long before that tragic, sunny morning.

And what is "the state" but an embodiment of the desire to be free of such insecurity. A desire for the always ultimately undeliverable promise of an identity beyond ambivalence, a foundation that holds, a ground that will not give away beneath one's feet. It is in this sense that "the state" is a non-thing, a never to be fully realized ideal. The practices discussed in the previous chapters are expressions of the promise for a stable and reproducible inside, a unified territorial identity that can be unproblematically distinguished from the outside. A world where Samuel Huntington can refer to "the same kind of people" confident that we will all know what he means, that these words are no more than a reflection of "reality."[10] A world where one's name can be placed on a "blacklist" because of the ethnic group to which one belongs and this justified in the name of security.[11] What all of the immigration practices in the United States, Britain, and France have in common is the goal of delivering on this promise and the ultimate impossibility of doing so. The dynamic nature of statecraft revolves around the promise and its failure. The perpetual tension. The practices examined in the preceding chapters are examples of the careful balancing of the tensions discussed in Chapters 1 and 2, that is, the tension between the schizophrenic and paranoiac poles of desire and between the principles of social protection and the phenomenon of globalization, which raises the issue of the boundaries of societies and the identities of those who belong and those who do not. Desire opens up a space whereby one engages in practices that simultaneously produce foundational grounds and render those grounds always in flux and never quite fixed.

I have offered an understanding of "the state" as a desire for order, a desire to overcome ambiguity and uncertainty. Such an understanding moves radically away from conceptualizations that reify "the state" as a completed accomplishment, a concrete entity, a closed totality. "The state," as desire, as the movement of desire adds a dynamic element to our understanding and expands the idea of statecraft to encompass all of the social realm, "from the head of the despot to the hearts of his subjects."[12] "The state" is an ideal that is never fully realized, but also never abandoned. The fact that it is never fully realized, by no means, makes it any less powerful or consequential. The opposite may actually be the case. Practices motivated by the desire of statecraft have often resulted in the curtailing of rights for immigrants, both legal and illegal, as the 1996 laws in the United States illustrate. In both the realms of official government and within society, practices of statecraft have been implicated in a contemporary form of racism that I (and others) have referred to as "neo-racism." The links between neo-racism and immigration are not identical in the cases examined in this study, though the idea of an inherent threshold of tolerance beyond which conflict becomes inevitable has been prominent in all three. The concept of "neo-racism" is an attempt to capture certain manifestations of the anxiety present in these responses. Balibar cautions that the term "neo-racism" only imperfectly expresses the new configurations that are not just variants of earlier racisms.[13] He suggests that the very word "race" and complements such as color, ethnicity, and so on are changing meanings today. However, I would suggest that the value of this term, lies in its very ability to capture (however imperfectly) this change. It enables us to conceptualize the contemporary articulation between racism and nationalism and while the defining feature of racism is not biological difference or skin color it does not necessarily preclude possible linkages between contemporary practices of exclusion and earlier constructions of difference, which were in fact anchored in perceptions of biological difference.

My purpose in this study has not been to compare the three cases as is conventionally understood in mainstream social science. Rather it has been to raise awareness of a multi-faceted phenomenon, that is, operative in Western countries today in response to immigration from Third World countries and to suggest an understanding of statecraft where insecurity and desire are central. Reflecting on this study, I am certain I have not done justice to the complex concept of desire and its implication in practices of statecraft and the numerous constructs associated with ideas about "the state" and international relations. Our academic international relations vocabulary is so full of concepts that we attempt to strip of all desire, to deny their passion, their lust, their taste, their color, and their feelings. But surely we must know that things like sovereignty and statecraft can only be made sterile and scientific and rigorous in the vigorously patrolled pages of journals fed by our own desires for secure grounds, words meant only for "us." Perhaps it is not words though, that ultimately will let us touch the desire we have such a hard time articulating. Perhaps studies, such as this one, can never do justice to desire. Perhaps all of our words are meant to deny desire. Perhaps we must do more, more to be sure than I have done here. Perhaps we must go to the edges ourselves, to those places where one world ends and another begins and both blur into one another. Perhaps we must stand at one of the many border areas of the world, like the Strait of Gibraltar, or the Sahara desert, or the deserts between the Southwestern United States and Mexico. "The Strait of Gibraltar today constitutes the largest mass grave in Europe," says Santiago Yerga, a lawyer at a church sponsored shelter in Cadiz, Spain who helps illegal immigrants get working papers.[14] "The big gate is the Sahara desert," says Joan Ignasi Soler of Doctors Without Borders.[15] Stand at the edge and look out over the vast emptiness – deathly still, threatening, beautiful. You wonder how many human beings are out there. How many bodies? Sovereignty, desire, statecraft. You can feel them in your bones. They resonate with the hot wind that blows across the land, around the mountains, through the arroyos. They stick in your mouth as you breathe in the desert dust. Watch a busload of "illegals" being dropped back at the border. Desire fills the air in places such as this. It whispers everything but rationality. It entices and promises and celebrates and denies. The bitter taste of statecraft.

Notes

1 Statecraft's desire and anti-immigrantism in Western democracies

1 Gilles Deleuze and Felix Guattari, 1983, *Anti-Oedipus – Capitalism and Schizophrenia*, translated by Robert Hurley, Mark Seem, and Helen R. Lane, Minneapolis: University of Minnesota Press, p. 154.
2 Perhaps the most recent addition to the array of perceived threats to US security is the spread of infectious disease. The National Intelligence Council argues that the infectious disease threat will complicate US and global security over the next twenty years, will endanger US citizens abroad and at home, will threaten US armed forces overseas, and will exacerbate political instability in key countries and regions. See "National Intelligence Estimate: The Global Infectious Disease Threat and Its Implications for the U.S." National Intelligence Council, January 2000, *Environment Report, Change and Security Project*, Issue 6, Summer, The Woodrow Wilson Center, pp. 33–65.
3 Abadan-Unat Nermin, 1987 used the term "new global reality" to describe international migration. Summary of the Main Results of Conference of OECD Working Party on Migration. *The Future of Migration*, Paris: OECD. Peter Stalker suggests that migration or the fear of it is closely connected with other aspects of globalization. See Peter Stalker, 2000, *Workers Without Frontiers – The Impact of Globalization on International Migration*, Boulder: Lynne Rienner Publishers.
4 Gilles Deleuze and Felix Guattari, 1983, *Anti-Oedipus – Capitalism and Schizophrenia*, translated by Robert Hurley, Mark Seem, and Helen R. Lane, Minneapolis: University of Minnesota Press, p. 29.
5 The conception of the state as a "unitary rational actor" in international relations scholarship is so prevalent as to almost constitute a defining feature of the discipline. In recent years the neorealism versus neoliberalism debate on relative versus absolute gains has also become one of the discipline's central debates.
6 Brian Massumi, 1996, *A User's Guide to Capitalism and Schizophrenia – Deviations from Deleuze and Guattari*, Cambridge and London: MIT Press, p. 8.
7 See *World Migration Report 2000*, International Organization for Migration, November 2000; Peter Stalker, 2000, op. cit., pp. 7, 26; SOPEMI, Continuous Reporting System on Migration. Trends in International Migration, 1992. Paris: Organization for Economic Cooperation and Development, p. 20.

8 See SOPEMI ibid., p. 41; Doris Meissner, Robert Hormats, Antonio Garrigues Walker, and Shijuro Ogata, 1993, *International Migration Challenges in a New Era. A Report to the Trilateral Commission.*

9 See *World Migration Report 2000,* International Organization for Migration, November 2000, English Press Kit.

10 *Migration News,* 2000, 7(11), Internet edition.

11 Quoted in Vaughn Bevan, 1986, *The Development of British Immigration Law,* London: Croom Helm, p. 85.

12 Myron Weiner, 1995, *The Global Migration Crisis – Challenge to States and Human Rights,* New York: Harper Collins.

13 Samuel P. Huntington, 1996, "The West: Unique, Not Universal," *Foreign Affairs,* 75(6), 28–46.

14 Arthur M. Schlesinger, Jr, 1992, *The Disuniting of America – Reflections on a Multicultural Society,* p. 17.

15 See Roger Cohen, "Europe's Love–Hate Affair With Foreigners," *The New York Times,* Weekly In Review section, 12/24/00, pp. 1, 6.

16 Max Silverman, 1992, *Deconstructing the Nation: Immigration, Racism and Citizenship in Modern France,* London: Routledge, p. 3 observes that in France the term "immigrant" is frequently used only to signify non-Europeans, especially Africans and those from the Caribbean resulting in the ironic situation where French nationals are often assumed to be immigrants while Spanish, Portuguese, and Italians are assumed to be French citizens. Robert Miles, 1993, *Racism After 'Race Relations',* London: Routledge, pp. 206–207 also notes the use of the term "immigrant" to refer only to those who originate from nation-states included in the "Third World" and who are characterized by cultural and somatic characteristics that constitute signs of difference. This is arguably the case for the United States as well.

17 Brimlow's book is examined in more detail in the next chapter.

18 For example, see Ian Clark, 1999, Eleonore Kofman and Gillian Youngs (eds), 1999, *Globalization – Theory and Practice,* London: Pinter; *Globalization and International Relations Theory,* Oxford: Oxford University Press.

19 James Rosenau, 1997, *Along the Domestic–Foreign Frontier: Exploring Governance in a Turbulent World,* London: Cambridge University Press, p. 44.

20 See Paul Kennedy, 1993, *Preparing for the Twenty-First Century,* New York: Random House, pp. 21–47; Kimberly Hamilton and Kate Holder, 1991, "International Migration and Foreign Policy: A Survey of the Literature." *The Washington Quarterly,* Spring, 195–196. The views of Huntington, Schlesinger Jr. and Weiner noted above are also consistent with this understanding of immigration as a threat to state sovereignty.

21 For examples of this argument see, Wayne Cornelius, Philip L. Martin, and James F. Hollifield (eds), 1994, *Controlling Immigration: A Global Perspective,* Stanford: Stanford University Press; Yasemin Soysal, 1994, *Limits of Citizenship: Migrants and Postnational Membership in Europe,* Chicago: University of Chicago Press; David Jacobson, 1996, *Rights Beyond Borders: Immigration and the Decline of Citizenship,* Baltimore: Johns Hopkins University Press. For an opposing view see the chapters in Peter Andreas and Timothy Snyder (eds), 1996, *The Wall Around the*

West – State Borders and Immigration Controls in North America and Europe, Boulder and New York: Rowman and Littlefield Publishers, Inc., 2000, see especially chapter 3, "States and the Regulation of Migration in the Twentieth-Century North Atlantic World," by John Torpey.

22 For a useful discussion of varying interpretations of globalization and its implications for "the state" see Ian Clark, 1999, op. cit., 1999; James F. Hollifield, 2000, "The Politics of International Migration – How Can We 'Bring the State Back In'," *Migration Theory – Talking Across Disciplines*, New York and London: Routledge; Leo Panitch, 1996, "Rethinking the Role of the State" in *Globalization – Critical Reflections*, James Mittelman (ed.), Boulder: Lynne Reinner.

23 Andreas and Snyder, op. cit., pp. 4, 9.

24 See Dan Malone, 2001, "Asylum Awaits Liberian Detained Six Years," *Washington Post*, January 21, Internet edition; Sharon L. Crenson, 2001, "Thousands of Refugees Jailed Under Immigration Law," *San Francisco Gate*, January 20, Internet edition.

25 See Peter Andreas, 2000, *Border Games – Policing the U.S.–Mexico Divide*, New York: Cornell University Presses. Andreas is referring specifically to border policing practices but his suggestion is more widely applicable.

26 I agree with William Connolly's suggestion that the flows and fixations of desire are "too protean, multiple, contingent, and promiscuous" for it to be defined in any positivistic way. See Connolly, 1995, *The Ethos of Pluralization*, Minneapolis: University of Minnesota Press, pp. 49–50.

27 Zygmunt Bauman, 1991, *Modernity and Ambivalence*, Cambridge, UK: Polity Press, p. 4.

28 Karl Polanyi, 1944, *The Great Transformation*, Boston: Beacon Press, p. 132.

29 Ibid., p. 73.

30 Colin Gordon, 1991, "Governmental Rationality: An Introduction," in *The Foucault Effect – Studies in Governmentality*, Graham Burchell, Colin Gordon, and Peter Miller (eds), Chicago: University of Chicago Press, pp. 21–22.

31 The term "effect" is important here. It implies that things like unity, identities, foundations are never given or fixed. They are never accomplished facts, but always in the process of being produced, being effected.

32 Gilles Deleuze and Felix Guattari, 1983, *Anti-Oedipus – Capitalism and Schizophrenia*, translated by Robert Hurley, Mark Seem, and Helen R. Lane, Minneapolis: University of Minnesota Press, p. 29.

33 Deleuze and Guattari, ibid., pp. 33, 49 use the term "socius." Philip Goodchild, 1996, *Deleuze and Guattari – An Introduction to the Politics of Desire*, London: Sage Publications defines socius as the "phantasm of social space" within which "presuppositions as to what being with others means."

34 William Connolly, 1995, *The Ethos of Pluralization*, Minneapolis: University of Minnesota Press, pp. 49–50.

35 Gilles Deleuze, 1977, "Nomad Thought," *The New Nietzsche*, New York: Delta, p. 146.

36 Gilles Deleuze and Felix Guattari, 1987, *A Thousand Plateaus – Capitalism and Schizophrenia*, translated by Brian Massumi, Minneapolis: University of Minnesota Press, p. 53.

37 Deleuze and Guattari, 1983, op. cit., pp. 195–196, 199.
38 Deleuze and Guattari make frequent use of the term "machine," especially "desiring machine," the point as I understand it being to place a continual emphasis on the notion of production, particularly the productive nature of desire. Capitalism, for Deleuze and Guattari is desiring production par excellance.
39 Deleuze and Guattaria, 1983, op. cit., pp. 246, 251–252.
40 Deleuze and Guattari, 1983, op. cit., pp. 220–221.
41 John Conroy, 2000, *Unspeakable Acts, Ordinary People – The Dynamics of Torture*, New York: Alfred A. Knopf.
42 *Amnesty International News*, 1995, 25(9).
43 Suzanne Daley, 1997, "Apartheid Torturer Testifies As Evil Show its Banal Face," *New York Times*, Internet edition.
44 See Amy Waldman, 1999, "The Diallo Shooting: The Overview; 4 Officers Enter Not-Guilty Please to Murder Counts in Diallo Case," *New York Times*, April 1, Internet edition. Numerous other articles on this case appear in the *New York Times*.
45 This is not really such a new idea. Others have pointed to the violence inherent in "the state." Julia Kristeva, 1991, *Strangers to Ourselves*, New York: Columbia University Press, p. 151 suggests that "The world of barbarity thus comes to a head in a single world composed of states, in which only those people organized into national residencies are entitled to have rights." Of course, as these example illustrate, even those organized into national residences are subject to the mark of the Urstaat. Marcuse suggests that advanced industrial societies are inherently repressive. See Herbert Marcuse, 1964, *One-Dimensional Man*, Boston: Beacon Press, and Alan Wolfe, 1978, *The Seamy Side of Democracy*, New York and London: Longman. My suggestion here though is broader, more inclusive than advanced industrial societies and economic interests do not necessarily form the basis for practices of statecraft. Because the perceived sources of disorder are so diverse, the desire for order springs from diverse locales with no predetermined base in class, race, gender, or other socially constructed groups. In other words, any group is subject to experiencing a violation or denial of rights if they or their activities are deemed a threat to order.
46 Policies such as Operation Gatekeeper force immigrants to travel through dangerously hot and cold deserts as well as through toxic rivers that border patrol agents will not go in. See "Churches Target Border-Crossing Deaths: Immigration Coalition Plans Emergency Water Stations After a Record Number of Migrants Perish in Hot Arizona Desert," (no author) *Los Angeles Times*, December 27, 2000 Internet edition; "Illegal Immigrants Brave Toxic River," *CBS Evening News*, July 23, 2000, Internet edition. See Roxanne Lynn Doty, 2001, "Desert Tracts: Statecraft in Remote Places," *Alternatives*, 26, 523–543.
47 See Julie Amparano, 1997, "Brown Skin: No Civil Rights?" *The Arizona Republic*, August 27, pp. A1, A14.
48 Deleuze and Guattari, 1987, *A Thousand Plateaus – Capitalism and Schizophrenia*, Minneapolis: University of Minnesota Press, pp. 427, 447.
49 Ibid., p. 448.
50 Deleuze and Guattari (1987: 449, 569) offer the example of the freed slaves in the Chinese Empire who formed the first seeds of private

property and trade. Marx and Engles noted that it was the Roman plebians who became the private owners of landed property and commercial industrial wealth precisely because they were excluded from all public rights.

51 Giovanna Procacci, 1991, "Social Economy and the Government of Poverty," in *The Foucault Effect – Studies in Governmentality,*" Graham Burchell, Colin Gordon, and Peter Miller (eds), Chicago: University of Chicago Press, pp. 151–169. The figure of the pauper is discussed in greater detail in the next chapter.

52 Kevin Cullen, 2000, "Europe's Unwelcome Mat," *Boston Globe,* December 28, Internet edition.

53 R. Jeffrey Smith, 2000, "Europe Bids Immigrants Unwelcome," *The Washington Post,* July 23, p. A01.

54 Roger Cohen, 2000, "Young Asian Knifed by German Neo-Nazis," *New York Times,* December 27, Internet edition; Jeevan Vasagar, 2000, "Three Sought for Racist Attack on Turk," *The Guardian Unlimited,* December 28, Internet edition.

55 Kate Connolly, 2000, "All Illegal Migrants Out, Says Haider," *Guardian Unlimited,* October 25, Internet edition.

56 Marlise Simons, 2000, "At Home, Resentment Hits Immigrants," *International Herald Tribune,* February 15, Internet edition; Emma Daly, 2000, "Riots in Spain's Vegetable Patch," *The Christian Science Monitor,* February 17, p. 6.

57 Charles Trueheart, 2000, "Fear of 'the Other' Fuels Rise of European Rightists" *International Herald Tribune,* December 12, Internet edition.

58 See Rena Singer, 2000, "South Africa's Brutal New Bias," *The Christian Science Monitor,* August 31, Internet edition; Greg Barrow, 2000, "South Africa's New Racism," *BBC News,* August 28, Internet edition.

59 Brian Massumi, op. cit., p. 7.

60 For example, see Philip Goodchild, 1996, *Deleuze and Guattari – An Introduction to the Politics of Desire,* London: Sage and Christopher Norris, 1992, *Uncritical Theory,* Boston: University of Massachusetts Press.

61 See Barbara Crossette, 2001, "Against a Trend, U.S. Population Will Bloom U.N. Says," *New York Times,* February 28, Internet edition.

62 See Chapter 4.

63 Swiss playwright Max Frisch quoted in Kitty Calavita, 1992, *Inside the State – The Bracero Program, Immigration and the I.N.S.,* New York, London: Routledge, p. 6.

64 Included here would be Richard Ashley, Cynthia Weber, R.B.J. Walker, James DerDerian, Michael Shapiro, David Campbell, James DerDerian, Siba Grovogui, Nevzat Soguk, and others who push the disciplinary boundaries of academic international relations.

2 Dangers and differences in a globalizing world

1 Jacques Derrida, 1974, *Of Grammatology,* translated by Gayatri Chakravorty Spivak, Baltimore: Johns Hopkins University Press, p. 143.

2 Philip Goodchild, 1996, *Deleuze and Guattari – An Introduction to the Politics of Desire,* London: Sage Publications, p. 96.

3 For example, see Charles Trueheart, "Fear of the 'Other' Fuels Rise of European Rightists," *The International Herald Tribune.* Referring to

immigration into Western Europe from North Africa, Turkey, and Eastern Europe, Trueheart quotes Patrick McCarthy, who teaches European studies at the Bologna campus of Johns Hopkins University, state, "The phenomenon has bred insecurity – the fear of losing your job, the fear of crime, the fear of 'the other'."

4 Stephen Castles (2000) points to the dilemma social scientists face in that "race" as no scientific basis, yet racial categorization is a crucial factor in social structure and action. See "The Racisms of Globalization," *Ethnicity and Globalization*, Sage Publications, p. 167.

5 For examples, see Greg Barrow, "South Africa's New Racism," *BBC News*, Internet edition, 8/28/00; Paul Salopek, 2001, "Intolerance in 'Rainbow Nation'," *The Chicago Tribune*, January 16, Internet edition.

6 Emma Daly, 2000, "Riots in Spain's 'Vegetable Patch'," *The Christian Science Monitor*, February 17, p. 6.

7 Jeevan Vasagar, 2000, "Three Sought for Racist Attack on Turk," *The Guardian Unlimited*, December 28, Internet edition.

8 Martin Barker, 1981, *The New Racism*, London: Routledge and Kegan Paul, p. 21.

9 Robert Miles critiques this definition as being too inclusive. He prefers to make the distinction between discourses, which construct differences as natural in order to exclude and discourses, which construct differences as natural "not only in order to exclude, but additionally, in order to marginalize a social collectivity within a particular constellation of relations of domination." See Miles, 1993, *Racism After 'Race Relations'*, London: Routledge, pp. 93–102. While Miles makes an important point, his definition ignores two significant issues. First, it imputes an intentionality behind discourse(s) when the power of discourse is often its relative autonomy, that is, it cannot be reduced to the intentions of either individuals or groups. Second, I would suggest that all too often exclusion and relations of domination go hand in hand. Differences are rarely constructed with the result being two separate but equal groups.

10 Pierre-Andre Taguieff, 1990, "The New Cultural Racism in France," *Telos*, No. 83, pp. 109–122.

11 Etienne Balibar, 1991, "Is There a Neo-Racism?" in *Race, Nation, Class – Ambiguous Identities*, Etienne Balibar and Immanuel Wallerstein (eds), London: Verso, pp. 59–60.

12 Howard Winant, 1994, *Racial Conditions*, Minneapolis: University of Minnesota Press, p. 101.

13 Colette Guillaumin (1991) discusses the appropriation by the new right of this type of discourse on difference whose roots lay in the anti-colonial and civil rights movements. See "Race and Discourse" in Max *Race, Discourse, and Power in France*, Silverman (ed.), Aldershot: Avebury, pp. 5–13.

14 Balibar, op. cit., p. 20.

15 I stress ostensibly here because, of course, segregation never actually meant anything even vaguely resembling "equality."

16 See Daniel Kanstroom, 1996, "Dangerous Undertones of the New Nativism," in *Immigrants Out! – The New Nativism and the Anti-Immigrant Impulse in the United States*, Juan F. Perea (ed.), New York University Press. Kanstroom points out that Spengler's racial theories were not entirely consistent over time and he actively promoted many of the same ideals as Hitler.

17 See Max Silverman, 1999, *Facing Postmodernity – Contemporary French Thought on Culture and Society*, London: Routledge, pp. 42–44.
18 See Kathryn A. Manzo, 1996, *Creating Boundaries – The Politics of Race and Nation*, Boulder: Lynne Rienner, pp. 50–53.
19 David Theo Goldberg, 1993, *Racist Culture – Philosophy and the Politics of Meaning*, London: Blackwell, pp. 70–74.
20 Michel Wierviorka, 1995, *The Arena of Racism*, London: Sage Publications, chapter 4.
21 Howard Winant (1994) suggests that the European experience which emphasizes culture resonates with developments in the United States "where neoconservatism has worked out the main axes of 'anti-racism' and where cultural difference arguments are daily becoming more central in racial discourse of all types." See *Racial Conditions*, University of Minnesota Press, pp. 101–102.
22 See Avtar Brah, 1996, *Cartographies of Diaspora – Contesting Identities*, London and New York: Routledge, pp. 166–170.
23 Taguieff, op. cit., p. 118.
24 See Anthony H. Richmond, 1994, *Global Apartheid – Refugees, Racism, and the New World Order*, Oxford: Oxford University Press, chapter 12.
25 See Peter Brimlow, 1995, *Alien Nation: Common Sense About America's Immigration Disaster*, New York: Random House. For detailed critiques of Brimlow's books and views on immigration see, Thomas Jackson, "Immigration: The Debate Becomes Interesting," Internet, http://www.amren.com/alienatin.htm; Jack Miles, 1995, "The Coming Immigration Debate," *The Atlantic Monthly*, April; Peter H. Schuck, 1996, "Alien Rumination: What Immigrants Have Wrought in America," *Yale Law Journal*, 105, 1963–2012.
26 See Brimlow, ibid., p. 68.
27 Eric Hobsbawm, 1992, *Nations and Nationalism Since 1780*, Cambridge: Cambridge University Press.
28 Samuel P. Huntington, 1993, "The Clash of Civilizations," *Foreign Affairs*, Summer, 22–49.
29 Samuel P. Huntington, 2001, "Migration Flows Are the Central Issue of Our Time" *International Herald Tribune*, February 2, Internet edition.
30 Ibid.
31 Samuel Huntington, 2000, "The Special Case of Mexican Immigration – Why Mexico Is a Problem." *American Enterprise*, December. http://www.theamericanenterprise.org/taedec00c.html, online edition A version of this article was also published by the Center for Immigration Studies, See Samuel P. Huntington, 2000, "Reconsidering Immigration – Is Mexico a Special Case?" Backgrounder, November, http://www.cis.org/articles/2000/back1100.html.
32 Ibid.
33 Michael Walzer, 1983, *Spheres of Justice*, New York: Basic Books, pp. 38–39.
34 Brimlow and Huntington is somewhat more obvious in this regard, though subtlety is not necessarily less benign.
35 Veit Bader suggests that the creation of Walzer's "common world of meaning" attributed to nation-states required an erasure of rival memories and histories so as to produce the dominant one. Internally, strategies of normalization and discipline have been applied in order to erase other

languages, to create religious homogeneity, and to crush competing cultures and frames of meaning and interpretation. See Bader, 1995, "Citizenship and Exclusion," *Political Theory*, 23(2), 211–246.

36 For a discussion of "race" that elaborates on its social constructedness and its relevance for international relations, see Roxanne Doty, 1993, "The Bounds of Race in International Relations," *Millennium – Journal of International Studies*, 22, 443–461.

37 Paul Gilroy, 1987, *There Ain't No Black in the Union Jack – The Cultural Politics of Race and Nation*, Chicago: University of Chicago Press, p. 39.

38 Etienne Balibar, 1991b, in Balibar and Wallerstein, op. cit., p. 54.

39 Silverman, op. cit., 333–349.

40 Cynthia Enloe, 1981, "The Growth of the State and Ethnic Mobilization," *Ethnic and Racial Studies*, 4(2).

41 I am borrowing here from Derrida's discussion of three forms of limits; the problematic closure, the anthropological border, and the conceptual demarcation. See Jacques Derrida, 1995, *Aporias*, translated by Thomas Dutoit, Stanford: Stanford University Press, pp. 40–42.

42 George Simmel, 1908, *On Individuality and Social Forms*, Chicago: University of Chicago Press.

43 Kristeva, op. cit., p. 1.

44 Bauman, op. cit., pp. 59, 71.

45 Colin Gordon, 1991, "Governmental Rationality: An Introduction," in *The Foucault Effect – Studies in Governmentality*, Graham Burchell, Colin Gordon, and Peter Miller (eds), Chicago: University of Chicago Press, pp. 37–38.

46 Giovanna Procacci, 1991, "Social Economy and the Government of Poverty," ibid. p. 163.

47 Ibid., p. 161.

48 Gordon, op. cit., p. 38.

49 Procacci, op. cit., p. 160. It is interesting to note that the construction of a social citizen conducive to society's production and consumption of wealth was/is not limited to the nineteenth century. Harvey notes that in 1916 Henry Ford sent social workers into the homes of his workers to ensure that the "new man" of mass production had the right kind of moral probity, family life, and capacity for prudent and rational consumption to live up to corporate needs and expectations/see David Harvey, 1992, *The Condition of Postmodernity*, Cambridge: Basil Blackwell, p. 126. Arguably modernization theory's notion of "traditional man" who must be transformed into "modern man" follows this same line of thinking.

50 See Homi Bhabha, 1990, "Dissemination: Time, Narrative and the Margins of the Modern Nation," in *Nation and Narration*, Homi K. Bhabha (ed.), London: Routledge, pp. 291–3222.

51 Gilles Deleuze and Felix Guattari, 1983, *Anti-Oedipus – Capitalism and Schizophrenia*, translated by Robert Hurley, Mark Seem, and Helen R. Lane, Minneapolis: University of Minnesota Press, pp. 242–243.

52 See Roxanne Doty, 1996, "The Double-Writing of Statecraft: Exploring State Responses to Illegal Immigration," *Alternatives*, 21(2), 171–189.

53 Zygmunt Bauman, 1991, *Modernity and Ambivalence*, Cambridge, UK: Polity Press, pp. 65–75.

54 See Peter Andreas, 2000, "Introduction," in *The Wall Around the West –
State Borders and Immigration Controls in North America and Europe*,
Peter Andreas and Timothy Snyder (eds), Boulder and New York: Rowman
and Littlefield, p. 2; Peter Andreas, 2000, *Border Games – Policing the
U.S.–Mexico Divide*, Ithaca and London: Cornell University Press, p. vii.
55 Bauman, op. cit., p. 66.
56 Anthony Richmond, 1994, *Global Apartheid: Refugees, Racism and the
New World Order*, Oxford: Oxford University Press, p. 206.
57 Bauman, op. cit., p. 70.
58 Jacques Derrida, 1992, *The Other Heading – Reflections on Today's
Europe*, translated by Pascale-Anne Brault and Michael B. Naas,
Bloomington: Indianna University Press, pp. 72–73.
59 Maxim Silverman, 1999, *Facing Postmodernity – Contemporary French
Thought on Culture and Society*, London: Routledge, p. 43.
60 Richmond, op. cit., pp. 156–157.

3 Mark your territory

1 Mexican Foreign Secretary, Jorge Castaneda, 2001, quoted in "A Plea to
Accept Immigrants," *International Herald Tribune*, March 31,
http://www.iht.com/articles/12091.html, Internet edition.
2 Gilles Deleuze and Felix Guattari, 1983, *Anti-Oedipus – Capitalism and
Schizophrenia*, Minneapolis: University of Minnesota Press, pp. 139, 142.
3 Wade Graham, 1996, "Masters of the Game – How The U.S. Protects the
Traffic in Cheap Mexican Labor," *Harpers*, July, 35–50.
4 Kitty Calavita, 1992, *Inside The State – The Bracero Program,
Immigration, and the I.N.S.*, New York: Routledge.
5 Michael Kearney, 1991, "Borders and Boundaries of State at the End of
Empire," *Journal of Historical Sociology*, 4(1).
6 The Bush Administration is currently considering plans to allow more than
three million Mexicans living illegally in the United States to earn perma-
nent legal residency. Any such plan would be part of a broader agreement
to expand guest worker programs. Proposals for such a plan are being
drawn up by a group headed by US Secretary of State Colin Powell,
US Attorney General John D. Ashcroft, Mexican Foreign Secretary Jorge
G. Castaneda, and Mexican Interior Minister Santiago Creel. See Thomas
B. Edsall, 2001, "Amnesty Proposal is Huge Gamble for Bush," *The
Washington Post*, July 16, Internet edition; Eric Schmitt, 2001, "Bush
Aides Weigh Legalizing Status of Mexicans in U.S.," *New York Times*, July
15, Internet edition; Greg Miller and Patrick J. McDonnell, 2001,
"Immigration Task Force to Urge Policy Overhaul," *The Los Angeles
Times*, July 15, wire service; Tom Zoellner, 2001, "Mexico Says Legalize
Crossers or No Deal," *The Arizona Republic*, June 22.
7 "Death on the Border" is becoming an all too common headline in
the national press. INS programs such as Operation Gatekeeper in
the San Diego area, Operation Hold the Line, and others have forced
people to cross the border in increasingly remote and dangerous places.
See Roxanne Lynn Doty, 2001, "Desert Tracts – Statecraft in Remote
Places," *Alternatives*, 26, 523–543. As a result of these policies and in
effect along side them is the Border Patrol's "Border Safety Initiative,"

which began in 1998 and is designed to, among other things, target hazardous areas where "migrants may become lost, abandoned or in distress due to difficult terrain and the willingness of smugglers to lead them into dangerous territory." Part of the Border Safety Initiative is the Border Patrol Search Trauma and Rescue (BORSTAR) team, which was first implemented in the Tucson and San Diego border sectors and is being expanded to the Yuma and El Centro sectors. See *Border Safety Initiative* document available from the INS website, http://www.ins.usdoj.gov. Also see news release from this website, INS, 2001, "U.S. and Mexico Announce Expanded Efforts to Save Migrant Lives – Binational Strategy Includes Intensified Focus on High Risk Areas," June 15.

 8 A third law, which has some implications for immigrants, especially in terms of deportable offenses was also passed in 1996, "The Anti-terrorism and Effective Death Penalty Act." My primary focus in this chapter is on the other two laws.

 9 See Michael Fix and Wendy Zimmerman, 1997, "Welfare Reform: A New Immigrant Policy for the United States," *The Urban Institute*, April, http://www.migration.ucdavis.edu.

10 Quoted in Wade Graham, 1996, "Masters of the Game – How the U.S. Protects the Traffic in Cheap Mexican Labor," *Harpers*, July, 35–50.

11 See Illegal Immigration Reform and Immigration Responsibility Act of 1996 (Pub. L. No. 104–208), Title I., http://www.fedpub.com/immigration/docs.toc and http://www.ins.usdoj/gov.

12 William Branigin, 1999, "Border Patrol Being Pushed to Continue Fast Growth," *Washington Post*, May 13, p. AO3; Mirta Ojita, 1998, "Change in Laws Sets Off Big Wave of Deportation," *New York Times*, December 15.

13 Gary Martin, 1999, "INS Deports Record Number of Undocumented Immigrants," *San Antonio Express*, January 8, online edition.

14 National Border Patrol Strategy, 2000, "Immigration and Naturalization Service," August 31, http://www.ins.usdoj.gov.

15 Ibid. These operations are part of the Border Patrol's prevention through deterrence strategy, which seeks to "elevate the risk of apprehension to a level so high that prospective illegal entrants would consider it futile to attempt to enter the U.S. illegally." They have become quite controversial with the rising number of border crossing deaths that result from people crossing in increasingly dangerous areas, particularly the southwestern deserts. Their "success" is also debatable. For example, border apprehensions in the San Diego Sector decreased from a high of 524,231 in FY 1995 to 151,681 in FY 2000. At the same time, however, apprehensions increased in the Tucson Sector from 139,473 in FY 94 to 616,346 in FY 2000. See "U.S. Border Patrol Apprehensions" 2001. FAX from Nicole Chulick, INS Office of Public Relations, April 19. The *San Diego Union Tribune*, reports that the INS has actually never used their $34 million, high-tech fingerprint program, IDENT, to evaluate the law-enforcement crackdown along the border. IDENT can help the INS determine whether arrested undocumented immigrants are felons, smugglers, or have frequently crossed the border illegally. The Government Accounting Office, which has recommended that the INS analyze information from IDENT, says that the agency has not carried out a "comprehensive, systematic

evaluation of the strategy's effectiveness in detecting and deterring aliens from entering illegally." See, Joe Cantlupe, 2001, "INS to Tap Database to Assess Border Strategy," *San Diego Union Tribune*, August 29, Internet edition. For an insightful historical study of Operation Gatekeeper, see Nevins, 2002.

16 Carleste Hughes, 2001, "Lives On Hold – American Greets Some Refugees From Oppressive Nations With Strict Incarceration in a Brick Building in Jamaica," *Newsday*, June 3, p. G6.

17 Sharon L. Crenson, 2001, "Thousands of Refugees Jailed Under Immigration Law," *Associated Press*, www.sfgate.com, January 20.

18 Ibid.; and Elizabeth Llorente, 2001, "Asylum Comes with Bars," *The Bergen Record*, January 28.

19 Leslie Casimir, 2001, "Deportations Soar – Up 164% Since Tough New Law," *New York Daily News*, February 7, online edition.

20 "Current Information Issues," 1997, *Migration News*, 4(4).

21 In June of 2001, the US Supreme Court issued two rulings in favor of immigrants and against aspects of the 1996 legislation. In the first decision the Supreme Court ruled that immigrant criminals with no country to accept them cannot be jailed indefinitely after they have served their sentence. In the second decision the Supreme Court ruled that legal immigrants convicted of certain crimes are entitled to a court hearing before they can be deported. See Susan Sachs, 2001, "Second Thoughts: Cracking the Door for Immigrants," *New York Times*, July 1, online edition; Linda Greenhouse, 2001, "Supreme Court Limits Detention in Cases of Deportable Immigrants," *New York Times*, June 29; Linda Greenhouse, 2001, "Justices Permit Immigrants to Challenge Deportations," *New York Times*, June 26.

22 Fix and Zimmerman op. cit. note that 40 percent of immigrants who receive SSI are disabled and that 64 percent of households headed by a non-citizen contain children. Under a US budget compromise reached on May 16, 1997, Congress and President Bill Clinton agreed to modify the 1996 welfare law to maintain SSI and Medicaid benefits for disabled legal immigrants who entered the United States before August 23, 1996 and those in the United States before this date who are disabled or become disabled in the future. The compromise did not restore Medicaid health care benefits to the children of poor legal immigrant, leaving in place the option of states to cut off this benefit. See "Immigrants and Welfare," 1997, *Migration News*, 4(6).

23 Fix and Zimmerman, op. cit.

24 "Research Perspective on Migration," 1996, *Carnegie Endowment for International Peace – International Migration Policy Project*, 1(1).

25 Ibid.

26 For example, Borjas and Hilton found that 10.8 percent of immigrant households use welfare defined as cash assistance only, but if non-cash assistance is included this figure jumps to 20.7 percent. However, researchers using individuals as the unit of analysis find that only 6.6 percent of immigrants use cash assistance programs. See Carnegie study, ibid.

27 See Carnegie study, op. cit.

28 Fix and Zimmerman, op. cit.

29 Noah Adams, 1998, "All Things Considered," *National Public Radio*, July 21.

30 Hector Tobar, 1998, "An Ugly Stain On City's Bright and Shining Plan, Raid: In A Roundup of Illegal Immigrants, Chandler, Arizona Snared Many U.S. Citizens Who 'Looked Mexican'," *Los Angeles Times*, December 28, Internet edition. Also see Julie Amparano, 1997, "Brown Skin: No Civil Rights?" *The Arizona Republic*, August 17, pp. A1, A14. A $35 million lawsuit was filed against the city of Chandler. The suit was settled in February 1999. The city of Chandler, admitting no guilt or responsibility for civil rights violations, agreed to pay $400,000 to twenty-one plaintiffs. See Mark J. Scarp and Krist Baxter, 1999, "Chandler Settles Roundup Lawsuit," *East Valley Tribune*, February 11, pp. A1, A14. A Justice Department ruling in April 2002 cleared the way for Attorney General John Ashcroft to declare that the state and local police departments have the power to enforce federal immigration laws. The state of Florida will become the first jurisdiction to enter into a policing partnership with the Justice Department. Such agreements are strongly opposed by some Latino organizations and civil rights groups. See Eric Schmitt, 2002, "Ruling Clears Way to Use State Police in Immigration Duty," *New York Times*, April 4; Lesley Clark, 2001, "Florida Police Seek Power to Arrest Illegal Immigrants – Opponents Wary of Racial Profiling," *The Miami Herald*, December 8.

31 Robert J. C. Young, 1995, *Colonial Desire – Hybridity in Theory, Culture, and Race*, London and New York: Routledge, p. 172.

32 Gilles Deleuze and Felix Guattari,1987, *A Thousand Plateaus*, translated by Brian Massumi, Minneapolis: University of Minnesota Press, p. 455.

33 Graham, 1996, *Harpers*.

34 Wayne Cornelius, 1996, "Economics, Culture, and the Politics of Restricting Immigration," *The Chronicle of Higher Education*, November 15, pp. B4–B5.

35 The Bureau of Labor Statistics reported in September, 2000 that the number of immigrant workers jumped to 15.7 million last year which was a 17 percent increase from three years earlier. Immigrant analysts estimate that nearly 5 million of these workers are illegal immigrants. See Steve Greenhouse, 2000, "Foreign Workers at Highest Level in Seven Years," *New York Times*, September 4.

36 Gilles Deleuze and Felix Guattari, 1983, *Anti-Oedipus – Capitalism and Schizophrenia*, translated by Robert Hurley, Mark Seem, and Helen R. Lane, Minneapolis: University of Minnesota Press, pp. 257–258.

37 Giovanna Procacci, 1991, "Social Economy and the Government of Poverty," in *The Foucault Effect – Studies in Governmentality*, Graham Burchell, Colin Gordon, and Peter Miller (eds), Chicago: University of Chicago Press, pp. 151–169. Quote from pp. 158–159.

38 Ibid.

39 Ibid.

40 This has begun to change somewhat in recent years as evident in union recruiting of illegal immigrants, the placement of water stations in dangerous desert crossings, as well as the recent Supreme Court decisions noted in Note 16.

41 Peter Skerry, 1996, "Missing the Boat – Immigration Law Demonizes Foreigners But Solves Little," *Washington Post*, October 20.

42 Timothy J. Dunn, 1996, *The Militarization of the U.S.–Mexico Border, 1978–1992*, Austin: The Center for Mexican American Studies.

43 Marianne Constable, 1993, "Sovereignty and Governmentality in American Immigration Law," *Studies in Law, Politics, and Society*, 13, 249–271.

44 CISNEWS, December 17, 1998.

45 See "The Possible Effect of the U.S. Crackdown on Illegal Immigrants is Rattling Growers," 1998. *Jan Hose Mercury News*, July 5.

46 See B. Lindsey Lowell and Roberto Suro, 2002, "How Many Undocumented: The Numbers Behind the U.S.–Mexico Migration Talks," *The Pew Hispanic Center*, March 21, p. 8.

47 Laurie P. Cohen, 1998, "Free Ride with Help from I.N.S.–U.S. Meatpacker Work Force," *Wall Street Journal*, October 15, pp. A1, A8.

48 See *Migration News*, 1998, "I.N.S. Sanctions, Detentions, Fees," October. This issue also reports of a poultry processor who was previously fined $52,000 for employing illegal immigrants on the Delmarva peninsular who agree to join Basic Pilot in exchange for an end to INS raids.

49 The AFL–CIO adopted its position on amnesty last year in an effort to reach out to immigrant workers as a source of growth for unions. On July 18, 2001, Mexican Foreign Secretary Jorge Castaneda addressed the hotel workers convention in Los Angeles and got a rousing ovation when he said illegal immigrants should be given legal status to prevent exploitation. See Steven Greenhouse, 2001, "In U.S. Unions, Mexico Find Unlikely Ally on Immigration," *New York Times*, July 19, Internet edition.

50 Passage of some form of amnesty does not mean an end to reterritorializing practices. Indeed, amnesty/legalization could be considered a form of reterritorializing itself.

51 Op. cit.

52 Peter Andreas, 2000, *Border Games – Policing the U.S.–Mexico Divide*, Ithaca: Cornell University Press.

53 See Michael Kamber, 2001, "Deadly Game – Crossing to the Other Side," *Village Voice*, April 18–24, online editions and Michael Kamber, 2001, "A Link in the Chain," *Village Voice*, April 11–17, online edition.

54 See Gloria Anzaldua, 1987, *Borderlands–La Frontera*, San Francisco, Spinsters/Aunt Lute Book Company, p. 3. The entire quote is as follows "The U.S.–Mexican border es una herida abierta where the Third World grates again the first and bleeds. And before a scab forms it hemorrhages again, the lifeblood of two worlds merging to form a third country – a border culture."

4 The empire comes home to Britain

1 Suzanne Daley, 2001, "Risking Death in the Chunnel for a Dream of Life in Britain," *New York Times*, March 15, pp. A1, A12.

2 Ibid. Also see Richard Ford, 2001, "Britain Faces Wave of Immigration," *The Times*, January 23, Internet edition; David Walker, 2001, "Welcome To Britain," *Guardian*, January 29, Internet edition.

3 See Julian Glover, 2000, "A Chance for a Real Debate," *The Guardian*, September 11, Internet edition. This dilemma is not limited to Britain. For example, *The Guardian* reports that if living standards in EU countries is not to fall, they may have to allow a sixtyfold rise in immigration. Even with the EU's enlargement to eastern Europe, the biggest source of

potential immigration is the Third World, mainly Africa and Asia. See Jonathan Steele, 2000, "Fortress Europe Confronts the Unthinkable," *Guardian Unlimited*, October 30, Internet edition. See also, "Immigration is Good News," 2000. *BBC News Online*, December 20, Internet edition.

4 See Jonathan Steele, ibid. See also Philip Martin and Jonas Widgren, 2002, "International Migration: Facing the Challenge," *Population Reference Bureau*. March.

5 The British Home Office reports that racist incidents reported to the police in the year 2000 rose 107 percent over the previous year. See "Huge Rise in Race Crime, Reveals Government," 2001. Special Report by the staff and agencies of *The Guardian Unlimited*, January 18, Internet edition.

6 See Lucian Kim, 2001, "Britain Wants a Wider Mote Around 'Fortress Europe'," Special to *The Christian Science Monitor*, February 22, Internet edition.

7 The movement of Jamaicans to Great Britain was increased by the passage in the United States of the Walter–McCarran Act in 1952. This act, also known as the Immigration and Nationality Act of 1952, reaffirmed the national origins quotas of the 1920s and added security provisions designed to make it nearly impossible for suspected subversives to enter the United States. It was seen by many as racist because the national origins quota gave the vast bulk of immigrant slots to peoples from northern and western Europe. The Act imposed severe restrictions on immigrants from the British West Indies resulting in the immigration of people from Jamaica, Barbados, and Trinidad and Tobago to Great Britain rather than the United States. See David M. Reimers, 1992, *Still the Golden Door – The Third World Comes to America*, New York: Columbia University Press, chapters 1 and 5; Jeannette Money, 1999, *Fences and Neighbors – The Political Geography of Immigration Control*, Ithaca and London: Cornell University Press, chapter 4.

8 See John Western, 1992, *A Passage to England*, Minneapolis: University of Minnesota Press, p. 77.

9 This act distinguished between Commonwealth citizens and citizens of the United States and colonies (CUKCs). Both had unrestricted rights of entry and residence in the United Kingdom. The term "Commonwealth" originally referred to the association of self-governing communities of the British Empire composed of the white settler states of Australia, New Zealand, Canada, and South Africa. As other parts of the empire became independent they too joined the Commonwealth but were generally referred to as "new Commonwealth" countries. See Vaughan Bevan, 1986, *The Development of British Immigration Law*, London: Croom Helm; Gary P. Freeman, 1979, *Immigrant Labor and Racial Conflict in Industrial Societies – The French and British Experiences*, Princeton: Princeton University Press; Jeannette Money, 1999, *The Political Geography of Immigration Control*, Ithaca: Cornell University Press, chapter 4.

10 See Joseph Frankel, 1975, *British Foreign Policy 1945–1973*, London: Oxford University Press, p. 204.

11 Recruitment of immigrant labor in the post Second World War Britain took three forms; (1) the recruitment of Polish workers, (2) European Volunteer Workers, and (3) immigration from the "new" Commonwealth

territories of the Caribbean, the Indian subcontinent, the Mediterranean, the Far East, and Africa. This third source was by far the largest and most significant in terms of subsequent social and political developments in Britain. See Roxanne Lynn Doty, 1996, "Immigration and National Identity: Constructing the Nation," *Review of International Studies*, 22, 235–255; Zig Layton-Henry, 1984, *The Politics of Race in Britain*, London: Allen and Unwin.

12 A 1982 article from the conservative *Salisbury Review*, quoted in John Solomon, 1993, *Race and Racism in Britain*, London: The MacMillan Press Ltd, p. 187.

13 From Margaret Thatcher's famous "swamping speech," quoted in *The Guardian*, January 31, 1978.

14 Cyril Osborne, House of Commons, August, 1961, pp. 1320–1321.

15 See Robert Miles and Annie Phizacklea, 1984, *White Man's Country – Racism in British Politics*, London, p. 41. More recently in 1986 visa controls were introduced for visitors from India, Pakistan, Bangladesh, Nigeria, and Ghana justified by the need to control illegal immigration from these five countries. This, despite the fact that only 222 out of 452,00 visitors from these countries became illegal immigrants in 1985. See Solomos, 1993, op. cit., p. 73.

16 From "The Tablet," quoted in House of Commons, December 5, 1958, p. 1563.

17 J. Vaughan-Morgan, 1965, House of Commons, March 23, p. 359.

18 Frank, Soskice, 1965, Secretary of State for the Home Department, House of Commons, May 3, 711, 93.

19 Avtar Brah tells of the case in Southall where white parents lobbied the Minister of Education during his local visit to their school in 1963. Within that year a policy of dispersal was adopted by the Southall Education Committee. See Brah, 1996, *Cartographies of Diaspora – Contesting Identities*, London: Routledge, pp. 22–23.

20 This has been attributed in large part to Enoch Powell's successful linking of the immigration issue to the question of race relations. See Robin Cohen, 1994, *Frontiers of Identity*, New York: Longhand, p. 53.

21 Fisher, 1961, House of Commons, November 16.

22 See Vaughan Bevan, 1986, *The Development of British Immigration Law*, London: Croom Helm. Gary P. Freeman, 1979, *Immigrant Labor and Racial Conflict in Industrial Societies. The French and British Experiences*, Princeton: Princeton University Press. Doty, 1996, op. cit.

23 See Mark Lattimer, 1999, "When Labour Played the Racist Card," *New Statesman*, January 22, Internet edition.

24 Ibid.

25 Ibid.

26 See ibid., James Walvin, 1984, *Passage to Britain – Immigration in British History and Politics*, London: Penguin Books, pp. 119–120; David Jacobson, 1997, *Rights Across Borders – Immigration and the Decline of Citizenship*, Johns Hopkins University Press, p. 89; Kristen Couper, 1989, "Immigration, Nationality, and Citizenship in the United Kingdom," *New Political Science*, 16/17, pp. 91–99.

27 See Brah, op. cit., p. 34.

28 See Kathryn Manzo, 1996, *Creating Boundaries – The Politics of Race and Nation*, Boulder: Lynne Reinner Publishers, pp. 117–120; Jeannette Money, 1999, *Fences and Neighbors*, Ithaca: Cornell University Press, p. 70.

29 There were two categories of patrials. (1) Citizens of Britain and its colonies who had citizenship by birth, adoption, naturalization, or registration in Britain or who were born of parents, one of whom had British citizenship by birth, or one of whose grandparents had such citizenship and (2) Citizens of Britain and its colonies who had at anytime settled in Britain and who had been ordinarily resident in Britain for five years or more. See Solomos, 1993, op. cit., p. 69 and Bevan, 1986, op. cit., p. 83.

30 Tom Reese, 1982, "Immigration Policies in the United Kingdom," in *Race in Britain – Continuity and Change*, Charles Husband (ed.), London: Hutchinson, p. 89.

31 House of Commons, 1987.

32 Three categories of citizenship were created by this act: (1) British citizens (those with close personal connection with the United Kingdom either because their parents or grandparents were born, adopted, naturalized, or registered as citizens of the United Kingdom or through permanent settlement, (2) citizens of British Dependent Territories (those who are British citizens because of their own or their parents' or grandparents' birth, naturalization or registration, and (3) British Overseas Citizens, a largely formal category with few privileges and no automatic right of entry. See Harry Goulborne, 1991, *Ethnicity and Nationalism in Post-Imperial Britain*, Cambridge: Cambridge University Press, p. 119; Zig Layton-Henry, 1985, *The Politics of Race in Britain*, London: Allen and Unwin, pp. 157–158; Freeman in Messina *et al.*, op. cit., pp. 26–27.

33 See British Parliamentary Debates, June 3, 1981, Volume 5, Col. 939.

34 See David Coleman, 1984, "Immigration Policy in Great Britain," in *Migration Policies: A Comparative Perspective*, F. Heckman and W. Bosswick (eds), Banberg, Germany: Enke, pp. 113–136 and Robin Cohen, 1994, *Frontiers of Identity*, New York: Longham, p. 65.

35 See Brah, 1996, op. cit., pp. 166–167.

36 Gary Younge, 2001, "The West Want the Free Movement of Capital, But Not of Labour. It Is Illogical and Immoral," *Guardian Unlimited*, March 19, Internet edition.

37 John Solomon, 1993, *Race and Racism in Britain*, London: The MacMillan Press Ltd, p. 121.

38 House of Commons Debates, Volume 585, p. 1422, April 3, 1958. Quoted in Roxanne Lynn Doty, 1996, "Immigration and National Identity: Constructing the Nation," *Review of International Studies*, 22, 235–255.

39 House of Commons Debates, Volume 634, p. 1967, February 17, 1961. Quoted in Doty, ibid.

40 Robin Cohen, 1994, *Frontiers of Identity*, New York: Longham, p. 126.

41 Cohen, op. cit., p. 126; Paul Gordon, 1985, *Policing Immigration*, London: Pluto Press, pp. 22–23.

42 See Paul Gordon, 1985, *Policing Immigration*, London: Pluto Press, pp. 14–24; Louis Kushnick points out that under the 1971 Act the police had the power to arrest anyone suspected of being an illegal entrant. See Louis Kushnick, 1998, *Race, Class and Struggle – Essays on Racism and Inequality in Britain, the US, and Western Europe*, London: Rivers Oram Press, p. 117.

43 Ibid., p. 60.
44 See Brah, 1996, pp. 38–39.
45 Solomon, 1993, p. 128.
46 Paul Gilroy, 1987, *There Ain't No Black in the Union Jack – The Cultural Politics of Race and Nation*, Chicago: University of Chicago Press, p. 89.
47 Ibid. pp. 72–113.
48 See Solomon, 1993, pp. 130–135.
49 See Walvin, 1984, p. 173.
50 Gilroy, op. cit., pp. 97–98.
51 See Paul Gilroy, 1987, *There Ain't No Black in the Union Jack – The Cultural Politics of Race and Nation*, Chicago: University of Chicago Press, chapter 3.
52 See "Black People More Likely to be Stopped and Searched," 2001, *ANONOVA*, January 18, http://www.anonova.com.
53 See "Killer Politics," CARF 60, February/March 2001.
54 A. Sivanandan, Director, Institute of Race Relations, 2001, "The Emergence of Xeno-Racism," *Institute of Race Relations*, July.
55 The number of asylum applicants in Britain for 2000 was 97,000, which was 22 percent of the total number of applicants in Europe. See Suzanne Daley, 2001, "Risking Death in the Chunnel For a Dream of Life in Britain," *New York Times*, March 15, pp. A1, A12. The percentage of asylum-seekers granted refugee status in 1999 was 12.1 percent with 102,870 cases still pending. See "Asylum Seekers: Europe's Dilemma," *BBC News*, February 2, online edition.
56 Daily Mail, March 1, 2000.
57 The British National Party (BNP) was formed in the 1980s as a result of split of the National Front (NF) into several fragments. The biggest was the BNP. The NF remains a tiny splinter group with less than 100 members. Merger talks between the BNP and the NF recently have failed. See "Keep The Nazis Out of Dover," 1999, online publication by the *Campaign Against Racism and Fascism*, http://www.canterbury.u-net.com/Dover.html.
58 On the events in Dover, see the following publications by the Campaign Against Racism and Facism, "Exclusion: New Labour Style," CARF 49, April/May 1999; "Stop this Bogus Tabloid Nationalism," CARF 55, April/May 2000. All of these publications are available on-line, http://www.carf.demon.co.uk.
59 See "The Dispersal of Xenophobia," A special report by the Institute of Race Relations, February 15, 2001, online edition.
60 "Exclusion: New Labour Style," published by the Campaign Against Racism and Facism, CARF, Vol. 49, April/May 1999, www.demon.co.uk, Internet edition.
61 In August, 2001, the new Home Secretary, David Blunkett, ordered a shakeup of the asylum dispersal policy after a Kurdish asylum-seeker was stabbed. See Gaby Hinsliff and Martin Bright, 2001, "Blunkett Orders Shake-Up in Dispersal of Refugees to Cities," *The Observer*, August 12, Internet edition.
62 See "Straw Proposes Asylum Blacklist," 2001. By the staff of *The Guardian Limited*, February 6, Internet edition.
63 See "Straw Targets 30,000 Would-Be Asylum Seekers," 2001. By the staff of *The Guardian Unlimited*, February 25, Internet edition.

64 Ian Burrell, Home Affairs Correspondent, 2001, "Home Office Draws Up 'Hit List' for Immigrants," *The Independent*, May 2, http://news.independent.co.uk, Internet edition.

65 After this incident, which was reported in the *New York Times* and *The Guardian*, the screening was stopped. British diplomats denied charges of racism and said the screenings had stopped because they were successful in virtually halting the "flood" of Czech asylum-seekers. Two weeks later, though, the screenings were resumed. See Peter S. Green, 2001, "Tryout at Prague Airport for British Asylum Policy," *New York Times*, August 5, p. A4; Peter S. Green, "After Protest, British Halt Screening of Travelers in Prague," *New York Times*, August 8, p. A4; Rebecca Allison, 2001, "Czechs Let U.K. resume Asylum Screening," *Guardian Unlimited*, August 23, Internet edition. Universal screening would be a blow to the Czech government, which is hoping to join the European Union in 2004.

66 See "Prison for Asylum Seekers," CARF 60, February/March 2001.

67 Sue Lloyd-Roberts, 2001, "Britain's Jailed Asylum Seekers," *Guardian Unlmited*, August 23, Internet edition. Britain's latest plan as of May 2002 is for three "refugee villages" in rural England. Under the plan, three sites at former Ministry of Defense base in central England will house 750 refugees while their cases are being processed. The sites will come complete with school and health facilities to ensure they do not place undue burdens on small local communities. The plan has been widely criticized. See Ed Cropley, 2002, "Britain Plans 'Refugee Villages' for Asylum Seekers," *Reuters*, May 14, online edition; Mark Oliver, 2002, "Downing Street Denies 'Dumping' Refugees," *Guardian Unlimited*, May 14, Internet edition; Alan Travis, 2002, "Minister Stirs Row Over Plans for 15 New Centres," *Guardian Unlimited*, May 15, Internet edition; Vikram Dodd, 2002, "Race Watchdog Is Ill Informed, Claims Minister," *Guardian Unlimited*, May 17, Internet edition.

68 Roy Hattersly, 2000, "Definition of a Notional Identity," *The Guardian*, November 13, Internet edition

69 The Report of the Commission on the Future of Multi-Ethnic Britain," sponsored by the Runnymede Trust, October 2000. See also Alan Travis, 2000, "British Tag is Coded Racism," *The Guardian Unlimited*, October 11, Internet edition.

5 Seuil de tolerance

1 This chapter first appeared as an article in *Millennium: Journal of International Studies*, 28(3), 1999, under the title of "Racism, Desire and the Politics of Immigration." Subsequent updates have been added to this chapter.

2 Jeffery Taylor, 2000, "Another French Revolution – In Marseilles, Europe Confronts Its North African Future," *Harpers*, November, 58–66.

3 Prime Minister Lionel Jospin, quoted in, Frank Viviano, 1999, "Europe Suddenly Doesn't Even Recognize Itself," *San Francisco Chronicle*, March 3, p. A1.

4 Taylor, op. cit.

5 Gary P. Freeman, 1979, *Immigrant Labor and Racial Conflict in Industrial Societies. The French and British Experiences*, Princeton: Princeton

University Press, p. 69; Maxim Silverman, 1992, *Deconstructing the Nation – Immigration, Racism and Citizenship in Modern France*, London: Routledge, pp. 40, 71.

6 Freeman, ibid., p. 70. The ONI was under the direct supervision of the Ministry of Labor. Bilateral agreements were negotiated with Italy in 1946 and 1951, West Germany in 1950, Greece in 1954, Spain in 1961, Morocco, Mali, Mauritania, Tunisia, and Portugal in 1963, Senegal in 1964, and Yugoslavia and Turkey in 1965. Each of these agreements specified the number of workers to be admitted to France each year, conditions of work that was guaranteed and the requirements for entry. See Freeman, p. 72. Citizens of the French overseas departments of Guinea, Guadeloupe, Martinique, and Reunion were considered French nationals as was Algeria and had the right to freely enter and stay in France. See Silverman, ibid., p. 41.

7 Quoted in Silverman, op. cit., p. 44. See also Emmanuel Vaillant, 1997, "Making Them Legal," *Le Monde Diplomatique*, November, Internet edition.

8 Freeman, op. cit., p. 77.

9 Karl Polanyi, 1994, *The Great Transformation*, Boston: Beacon Press, p. 73.

10 Freeman, op. cit., p. 83.

11 France officially put into effect a ban on all primary immigration in 1974. This is still in effect today. Economic reasons were used to justify this, for example, the 1973 Middle East War and sharp rise in oil prices sparking fears over the prospects for economic growth, fears of rising unemployment and recession. Another justification though was that strict control was essential for the integration of those immigrants already in France. The ban on immigration originally applied to family reunification also, but this proved unworkable and in 1978 the Conseil d'Etat, France's highest administrative court, declared it to be unlawful. See Alec G. Hargreaves, 1995, *Immigration, Race, and Ethnicity in Contemporary France*, London: Routledge, p. 18.

12 Hargreaves ibid., p. 193. Postal-Vinay resigned in July when it became clear that his housing proposals would not receive the required funding. He was replaced by Paul Dijiud and later by Lionel Stoleru in 1977.

13 Ibid., p. 195.

14 Ibid., p. 339.

15 See Chapter 2, Note 35.

16 Freeman, op. cit., p. 157. The term was first used in 1964 by a sociologist investigating conflicts between Algerian families from the bidonvilles and French families from Parisian slums both of whom had been rehoused in a housing estate. See Robin Cohen, 1994, *Frontiers of Identity: The British and the Others*, London: Longman, p. 177.

17 In July of 1968 several measures were taken to clamp down on immigration. France unilaterally limited to 1,000 per month the number of Algerians who could enter the country to work. This was a significant reduction from the figures set by a 1964 agreement with Algeria, which had set the number at 50,000 per year. See Freeman, op. cit., p. 86. This number was subsequently set at 35,000 per year by the Franco–Algerian agreement of 1968. See Silverman, op. cit., p. 48.

18 Freeman, op. cit., p. 87; Hargreaves, op. cit., p. 216.

19 Freeman, op. cit., p. 88.
20 Quoted in Freeman, op. cit., p. 158.
21 Quoted in Neil MacMaster, 1991, "The 'Seuil de Tolerance': The Uses of a 'Scientific' Racist Concept," in *Race, Discourse, and Power in France,* Maxim Silverman (ed.), Aldershot: Gower, pp. 14–28.
22 Silverman, 1992, op. cit., p. 95.
23 From *Liberation,* January 12, 1990. Quoted in Silverman, 1992, op. cit., p. 96.
24 Silverman, 1992, op. cit., p. 96.
25 Hargreaves, 1995, p. 19.
26 Silverman, 1992, op. cit., p. 342.
27 "France Amends 1993 Immigration Law," *Migration News,* December 1996, 3(12).
28 Balibar, "Is There a Neo-Racism," p. 25.
29 The FN was formed in 1972 amidst increasing anti-immigrant sentiment. The FN and its leader Jean-Marie Le Pen played a central role in defining the debate on immigration. See Jonathan Marcus, 1995, *The National Front and French Politics,* Basingstoke: Macmillan, p. 80. In 1984, Le Pen and nine other FN candidates won seats in the European Parliament. In 1986, the FN also won thirty-five seats in the French National Assembly. See Cathie Lloyd and Hazel Waters, 1991, "France: One Culture, One People," *Race and Class,* 32(3), 49–65.
30 Frances Webber, 1991, "From Ethnocentrism to Euro-Racism," *Race and Class,* 32(3), 11–17.
31 Christian E. O'Connell, 1996, "Plight of France's *Sans-Papiers* Gives a Face to Struggle Over Immigration," *The Human Rights Brief*; Hargreaves, 1995, *Immigration, Race and Ethnicity in Contemporary France,* London: Routledge, pp. 173–177.
32 See Philippe Naughton, April 11, 1996, Mark Krikorian, immigration news letter. Also see Maurice Glele-Ahanhanzo, Report of the Special Rapporteur, "Elimination of Racism and Racial Discrimination – Measures to Combat Contemporary Forms of Racism, Racial Dsicrimination, Xenophobia and Related Intolerance," Fifty-first session, August 20, 1996, www.unhcr.ch.
33 The group of immigrants first attracted attention in March 1996 when they occupied the Saint-Ambrose church in Paris to demand residence papers. They were quickly evicted without incident and a small number were deported.
34 O'Connell, ibid. Also see "French Police Remove Immigrants from Church," *Migration News,* 1996, 3(9).
35 Sami Nair, 1996, "France: A Crisis of Integration," *Dissent,* 43(3). Also see "France Amends 1993 Immigration Law," *Migration News,* 1996, 3(12).
36 Shelese Emmons, 1997, "The Debre Bill: Immigration Legislation of a National Front," *Indiana Journal of Global Legal Studies,* 5(1), online edition.
37 Originally a draft proposal of the law had proposed that anyone receiving a visit by a foreigner had to report this to the local town hall or be charged with aiding and abetting illegal residency. Massive protests on the part of writers, artists, scientists, university teachers, journalists, etc. led to the withdrawal of this proposal and shifted the responsibility for reporting to

the immigrants themselves. See Mogniss H. Abdallah, 1999. "The Sans Papier Movement – A Climax in the History of French Immigration," July, *No Border Network,* http://www.noborder.org.
38 "France: Immigration Reform Approved," *Migration News*, March, 1997 4(3).
39 "France Amends Immigration Law," *Migration News*, 1997, 4(4).
40 "France: Repeal Immigration Laws." *Migration News*, 1997, 4(7).
41 The new laws, law number 98-349, took effect on May 11, 1998.
42 "French Immigration Bill," *Migration News*, 1997, 4(12); "France: Law, National Front," *Migration News*, 1998, 5(4).
43 "France: 70,000 Get Amnesty," *Migration News*, 5(7), 1998 and "France: Vatican, Politics." *Migration News*, 1998 5(9).
44 See earlier quote.
45 Charles Bremner, 2002. "Le Pen is Still Exuding that Right-Wing Menace", *The Times*, March 8, online edition.
46 "France: Le Pen," 2002. *Migration News*, May. This was the first time since 1969 that the left failed to reach the second round of the presidential elections and the first time a far right candidate came so close to power. Le Pen defeated the socialist prime minister, Lionel Jospin who finished third. See Staff, 2020. "What the French Papers Say", *Guardian Unlimited*, April 22, 2002 and Staff, 2002. "Shock French Election Result Sparks Protests", *Guardian Unlimited*, April 22, Internet edition.
47 Suzanne Daley, 2002. "Why Vote For Le Pen?", *International Herald Tribune*, April 26, Internet edition. Interview with a butcher in Gisgors, France who wanted to remain anonymous.
48 The National Front splintered into competing factions in December 1998. Le Pen dismissed the deputy leader Bruno Megret, who had forged alliances with conservative politicians from the mainstream parties in five of the twenty-two regional assemblies after the Socialists gained in March 1998 elections. See "France: National Front," 1999. *Migration News*, 6(1). Megret was elected to head a new FN, the National Movement Party. See "France: National Front, Headscarves," 1999. *Migration News*, 6(2).
49 Philippe Lheronde, a plumber who lives in Gisors, France where fewer than 2 percent of the inhabitants are immigrants. Quoted in Suzanne Daley, 2002, "Why Vote for Le Pen?" *New York Times*, April 26, online edition.
50 "France, Netherlands: Le Pen, Pim Fortuyn," 2002, *Migration News*, May.
51 Staff, 2002, "Sangatte Refugee Camp," *Guardian Unlimited*, May 23, Internet edition; Ben Russell and Nigel Moris, 2002, "France Agrees to Plan Timetable for Closing Sangatte Camp, *The Independent*, June 26, Internet edition.
52 Frank Viviano, 1999, op. cit., Jeffrey Tayler, 2000, op. cit.
53 Charles Trueheart, 2000, "Racism Persists Despite Egalitarian Creed," *Washington Post*, March 6, p. A25.
54 Viviano, op. cit.
55 Silverman, op. cit., p. 121.

6 In closing and reflection

1 Shehnaz Suterwalla, with Barbie Nadeau, Emma Daly, Rita O'Reilly, Christian Caryl, and Stefan Theil, 2001, "Immigration and Reality – Europe

has a Choice: Abandon Zero Immigration or Let Its Labor Market Suffer," *Newsweek*, web exclusive, January 28. http://www.msnbc.com/news/522494.asp?cp1=1.

2 British Foreign Secretary, Jack Straw, quoted in "E.U.: Illegal Immigation, Labor," *Migration News*, May 2002.

3 Cornelius Castoriadis, 1992, "Reflections on Racism," *Thesis Eleven*, No. 32, pp. 1–12.

4 Kevin Johnson, 2001, "Va. Group Accused of Illegal Efforts for Racist U.K. Party," *USA Today*, September 2, p. 4A. See Southern Poverty Law Center's Intelligence Reports, 2001, "Hand Across the Water," Fall, No. 103; "Blood on the Border," 2001, Spring, No. 101.

5 See Marie-Louise Moller, 2002, "Focus-Tough Immigration Policies Won't Work," *Reuters*, www.reuters.co.uk, online edition.

6 "Australian Troops Board Refugee Ship," 2001, *New York Times*, August 29, Internet edition; "Six African Immigrants Found Dead on Spain Beaches," 2001, www.CNN.com July 15; Jerome Socolovsky, 2001, "Nine Miles to a Better Life," *Chicago Sun Times*, August 19, Internet edition; Bruce Stanley, 2001, "Illegal Immigrants Plague Chunnel," *Washington Post*, August 24, Internet edition; Nicholas Le Quesne, 2001, "Just Within Reach," *Time – Europe*, September 2, Internet edition.

7 Maria Margaronis, 2001, "Europe's Unwelcome Guests," *The Nation*, May 27, pp. 14–20.

8 Ian Black, 2002, "Pim is dead...," *Guardian Unlimited*, May 17.

9 Steven Erlanger, 2002, "Europe's Identity Crisis," *New York Times*, May 2.

10 Quoted in Chapter 2.

11 See Chapter 4.

12 Gilles Deleuze and Felix Guattari, 1983, translated by Robert Hurley, Mark Seem, and Helen R. Lane, Minneapolis: University of Minnesota Press, p. 221.

13 Etienne Balibar, 1991, "Racism and Politics in Europe Today," *New Left Review*, No. 186, March/April, pp. 5–19.

14 Jerome Socolovsky, 2001, "Nine Miles to Better Life," *Chicago Sun Times*, August 19.

15 Keith B. Richburg, 2001, "At Spain's Gate, Africans Dream of Europe," *Washington Post*, March 28, p. A01.

Bibliography

Abdallah, Mogniss H., 1999, "The *San Papier* Movement – A Climax in the History of French Immigration," *No Borders Network*, July, http://www.noborder.org.

Adams, Noah, 1998, "All Things Considered," *National Public Radio*, July 21.

Allison, Rebecca, 2000, "Czechs Let U.K. Resume Asylum Screening," *Guardian Unlimited*, August 23, Internet edition.

Amnesty International News, 1995, 25(9).

Amparano, Julie, 1997, "Brown Skin: No Civil Rights?" *The Arizona Republic*, August 17, pp. A1 and A14.

ANANOVA, 2001, "Black People More Likely to be Stopped and Searched," January 18, http://www.ananova.com.

Andreas, Peter, 2000, *Border Games – Policing the U.S.–Mexico Divide*, Ithaca: Cornell University Press.

Andreas, Peter and Timothy Snyder (eds), 2000, *The Wall Around the West – State Borders and Immigration Controls in North America and Europe*, Oxford, UK and Lanhan, Maryland: Rowman and Littlefield Publishers, Inc.

Anzaldua, Gloria, 1987, Borderlands – La Fruntera, San Fransisco, Spinsters/ Aunt Lute Book Company.

Bader, Veit, 1995, "Citizenship and Exclusion," *Political Theory*, 23(2), 211–246.

Balibar, Etienne, 1991a, "Is There a Neo-Racism," in *Race, Nation, Class – Ambiguous Identities*, Immanuel Walleistein and Etienne Balibar (eds), London: Verso.

Balibar, Etienne, 1991b, "Racism and Nationalism," ibid.

Balibar, Etienne, 1991c, "Racism and Politics in Europe Today," *New Left Review*, No. 186, March/April, 5–19.

Barker, Martin, 1981, *The New Racism*, London: Routledge and Kegan Paul.

Barrow, Greg, 2000, "South Africa's New Racism," *BBC News*, August 28, Internet edition.

Bauman, Zygmunt, 1991, *Modernity and Ambivalence*, Cambridge, UK: Polity Press.

BBC News Online, 2000, "Immigration is Good News," December 28.

BBC News Online, 2001, "Asylum Seekers: Europe's Dilemma," February 6.

Bevan, Vaughan, 1986, *The Development of British Immigration Law*, London: Croom Helm.

Bhabha, Homi, 1990, "Dissemination: Time, Narrative, and the Margins of the Modern Nation," in *Nation and Narration*, Homi K. Bhabha (ed.), London: Routledge, pp. 291–322.

Black, Ian, 2002, "Pim is Dead...," *Guardian Unlimited*, May 17.

Brah, Avtar, 1996, *Cartographies of Diaspora – Contesting Identities*, London and New York: Routledge.

Branigin, William, 1999, "Border Patrol Being Pushed to Continue Fast Growth," *Washington Post*, May 13, p. A03.

Bremmer, Charles, 2002, "Le Pen is Still Exuding that Right-Wing Menace," *The Times*, March 8, online edition.

Brimlow, Peter, 1995, *Alien Nation: Common Sense About America's Immigration Disaster*, New York: Random House.

British Parliamentary Debates, 1981, June 3, Vol. 5, Col. 939.

Burrell, Ian, 2001, "Home Office Draws Up 'Hit List' for Immigrants," *The Independent*, May 2, Internet edition, http://www.news.independent.co.uk.

Calavita, Kitty, 1992, *Inside the State – The Bracero Program, Immigration and the I.N.S.*, New York, London: Routledge.

Campaign Against Racism and Fascism, 1999, "Exclusion: New Labour Style," CARF 49, April/May.

Campaign Against Racism and Fascism, No Date, "Keep the Nazis Out of Dover," http://www.canterbury.u-net.com/Dover.html.

Cantlupe, Joe, 2001, "INS to Tap Database to Assess Border Strategy," *San Diego Union Tribune*, August 29, Internet edition.

CARF 55, 2000, "Stop this Bogus Tabloid Nationalism," April/May.

CARF 60, 2001, "Killer Politics," February/March.

CARF 60, 2001, "Prison for Asylum Seekers," February/March.

Casimir, Leslie, 2001, "Deportations Soar-Up 164% Since Tough New Law," *New York Daily News*, February 7, online edition.

Castles, Stephen, 2000, *Ethnicity and Globalization. From Migrant Worker to Transnational Citizen*, London: Sage Publications.

Castoriadis, Cornelius, 1992, "Reflections on Racism," *Thesis Eleven*, No. 32, pp. 1–12.

CBS Evening News, 2000, *Immigrants Brave Toxic River*, July 23, Internet edition.

Clark, Ian, 1999, *Globalization and International Relations Theory*, London: Oxford University Press.

CNN.com, 2001, "Six African Immigrants Found Dead on Spain Beaches," July 15.

Cohen, Laurie P., 1998, "Free Ride with Help from INS–U.S. Meatpacker Work Force," *Wall Street Journal*, October 15, pp. A1 and A8.

Cohen, Robin, 1994, *Frontiers of Identity: The British and the Others*, London and New York: Longman.

Cohen, Roger, 2000, "Europe's Love–Hate Affair With Foreigners," *New York Times*, December 24, pp. 1–6.

Cohen, Roger, 2000, "Young Asian Knifed by German Neo-Nazis," *New York Times*, December 27, Internet edition.

Coleman, David, "Immigration Policy in Great Britain," in *Migration Policies: A Comparative Perspective*, F. Heckman and W. Bosswick (eds), Banberg, Germany: Enke, pp. 113–136.

Connolly, Kate, 2000, "All Illegal Migrants Out, Says Haider," *The Guardian Unlimited*, October 25, Internet edition.

Connolly, William, 1995, *The Ethos of Pluralization*, Minneapolis: University of Minnesota Press.

Conroy, John, 2000, *Unspeakable Acts, Ordinary People – The Dynamics of Torture*, New York: Alfred A. Knopf.

Constable, Marianne, 1993, "Sovereignty and Governmentality in American Immigration Law," *Studies in Law, Politics, and Society*, 13, 249–271.

Cornelius, Wayne, 1996, "Economics, Culture, and the Politics of Restricting Immigration," *The Chronicle of Higher Education*, November 15, pp. B4–B5.

Cornelius, Wayne, Phillip L. Martin, and James F. Hollifield (eds), 1994, *Controlling Immigration: A Global Perspective*, Stanford, CA: Stanford University Press.

Couper, Kristen, 1989, "Immigration, Nationality, and Citizenship in the United Kingdom," *New Political Science*, 16/17, 91–99.

Crenson, Sharon L., 2001, "Thousands of Refugees Jailed Under Immigration Law," *San Francisco Gate*, Stanford, Calif, January 20, Internet edition.

Cropley, Ed, 2002, "Britain Plans 'Refugee Villages' for Asylum Seekers," *Reuters*, May 14, online edition.

Crossetter, Barbara, 2001, "Against a Trend, U.S. Population Will Bloom U.N. Says," *New York Times*, February 28, Internet edition.

Cullen, Kevin, 2000, "Europe's Unwelcome Mat," *Boston Globe*, December 28, Internet edition.

Daley, Suzanne, 1997, "Apartheid Torturer Testifies As Evil Shows Its Banal Face," *New York Times*, November 9, Internet edition.

Daley, Suzanne, 2001, "Risking Death in the Chunnel for a Dream of Life in Britain," *New York Times*, March 15, pp. A1 and A12.

Daley, Suzanne, 2002, "Why Vote For Le Pen?" *The New York Times*, April 26, online edition.

Daly, Emma, 2000, "Riots in Spain's Vegetable Patch," *The Christian Science Monitor*, February 17, p. 6.

Deleuze, Gilles, 1977, "Nomad Thought," in *The New Nietzsche*, New York: Delta.

Deleuze, Gilles and Felix Guattari, 1983, *Anti-Oedipus – Capitalism and Schizophrenia*, translated by Robert Hurley, Mark Seem, and Helen R. Lane, Minneapolis: University of Minnesota Press.

Deleuze, Gilles and Felix Guattari, 1987, *A Thousand Plateaus – Capitalism and Schizophrenia*, translated by Brian Massumi, Minneapolis: University of Minnesota Press.

Derrida, Jacques, 1974, *Of Grammatology*, translated by Gayatri Chakravorty Spivak, Baltimore, MA: Johns Hopkins University Press.

Derrida, Jacques, 1992, *The Other Heading – Reflections on Today's Europe*, translated by Pascale-Anne Brault and Michael B. Naas, Bloomington: Indiana University Press.

Derrida, Jacques, 1995, *Aporias*, translated by Thomas Dutoit, Stanford: Stanford University Press.

Dodd, Vikram, 2002, "Race Watchdog is Ill Informed, Claims Minister," *Guardian Unlimited*, May 17.

Doty, Roxanne Lynn, 1993, "The Bounds of Race in International Relations," *Millennium-Journal of International Studies*, 22, 443–461.

Doty, Roxanne Lynn, 1996, "The Double-Writing of Statecraft: Exploring State Responses to Illegal Immigration," *Alternatives*, 21(2), 171–189.

Doty, Roxanne Lynn, 1996, "Immigration and National Identity: Constructing the Nation," *Review of International Studies*, 22, 235–255.

Doty, Roxanne Lynn, 2001, "Desert Tracts: Statecraft in Remote Places," *Alternatives*, 26, 523–543.

Dunn, Timothy J., 1996, *The Militarization of the U.S.–Mexico Border, 1978–1992*, Austin: The Center for Mexican American Studies.

Edsall, Thomas B., 2001, "Amnesty Proposal is Huge Gamble for Bush," *The Washington Post*, July 16, Internet edition.

Emmons, Shelese, 1997, "The Debre Bill: Immigration Legislation of a National Front," *Indiana Journal of Global Legal Studies*, Fall, 5(1), online edition.

Enloe, Cynthia, 1981, "The Growth of the State and Ethnic Mobilization," *Ethnic and Racial Studies*, 4(2).

Erlanger, Steven, 2002, "Europe's Identity Crisis," *The New York Times*, May 2.

Fisher, 1961, *House of Commons*, November 16.

Fix, Michael and Wendy Zimmerman, 1997, "Welfare Reform: A New Immigrant Policy for the United States," *The Urban Institute*, http://www.migration.ucdavis.edu.

Ford, Richard, 2001, "Britain Faces Wave of Immigration," *The Times*, January 23, Internet edition.

Frankel, Joseph, 1975, *British Foreign Policy 1945–1973*, London: Oxford University Press.

Freeman, Gary P., 1979, *Immigrant Labor and Racial Conflict in Industrial Societies. The French and British Experiences*, Princeton: Princeton University Press.

Gilroy, Paul, 1987, *There Ain't No Black in the Union Jack – The Cultural Politics of Race and Nation*, Chicago: University of Chicago Press.

Glele-Ahanhanzo, Maurice, 1996, *Elimination of Racism and Racial Discrimination – Measures to Combat Contemporary Forms of Racism, Racial Discrimination, Xenophobia and Related Intolerance*, Report of the Special Rapporteur, Fifty-First Session.

Glover, Julian, 2000, "A Chance for a Real Debate," *The Guardian*, September 11, Internet edition.

Goldberg, David Theo, 1993, *Racist Culture – Philosophy and the Politics of Meaning*, Oxford, UK and Cambridge, US: Blackwell.

Goodchild, Philip, 1996, *Deleuze and Guattari – An Introduction to the Politics of Desire*, London: Sage Publications.

Gordon, Colin, 1991, "Governmental Rationality: An Introduction," in *The Foucault Effect – Studies in Governmentality*, Graham Burchell, Colin Gordon and Peter Miller (eds), Chicago: University of Chicago Press.

Gordon, Paul, 1985, *Policing Immigration*, London: Pluto Press.

Goulborne, Harry, 1991, *Ethnicity and Nationalism in Post-Imperial Britain*, Cambridge: Cambridge University Press.

Graham, Wade, 1996, "Masters of the Game – How the U.S. Protects the Traffic in Cheap Mexican Labor," *Harpers*, July, 35–50.

Green, Peter S., 2001, "Tryout at Prague Airport for British Asylum Policy," *New York Times*, August 5, p. A4.

Green, Peter S., 2001, "After Protest, British Halt Screening of Travelers in Prague," *New York Times*, August 8, p. A4.

Greenhouse, Linda, 2001, "Justices Permit Immigrants to Challenge Deportations," *New York Times*, June 26, online edition.

Greenhouse, Linda, 2001, "Supreme Court Limits Detention in Cases of Deportable Immigrants," *New York Times*, June 29.

Greenhouse, Steve, 2000, "Foreign Workers at Highest Level in Seven Years," *New York Times*, September 4.

Greenhouse, Steven, 2001, "In U.S. Unions, Mexico Find Unlikely Ally on Immigration," *New York Times*, July 19, Internet edition.

Guardian Unlimited, 2001, "Huge Rise in Race Crime, Reveals Government," January 18, Internet edition.

Guardian Unlimited, 2001, "Straw Proposes Asylum Blacklist," February 6, Internet edition.

Guardian Unlimited, 2001, "Straw Targets 30,000 Would-Be Asylum Seekers," April 25, Internet edition.

Guardian Unlimited, 2002, "Shock French Election Result Sparks Protests," April 22, Internet edition.

Guardian Unlimited, 2002, "What the French Papers Say," April 22, Internet edition.

Guillaumin, Colette, 1991, "Race and Discourse," in *Race, Discourse, and Power in France*, Max Silverman (ed.), Aldershot: Avebury, pp. 5–13.

Hamilton, Kimberly and Kate Holder, 1991, "International Migration and Foreign Policy: A Survey of the Literature," *The Washington Quarterly*, Spring, 195–196.

Hargreaves, Alec G., 1995, *Immigration, Race and Ethnicity in Contemporary France*, London: Routledge.

Harvey, David, 1992, *The Condition of Postmodernity*, Oxford, UK: Basil Blackwell.

Hattersly, Roy, 2000, "Definition of a Notional Identity," *The Guardian*, November 13, Internet edition.

Hinsliff, Gaby and Martin Bright, 2001, "Blunkett Orders Shake-Up in Dispersal of Refugees to Cities," *The Observer*, August 12, Internet edition.

Hobsbawm, Eric, 1992, *Nations and Nationalism Since 1780*, Cambridge: Cambridge University Press.

Hollifield, James F., 2000, "The Politics of International Migration-How Can We 'Bring the State Back In'," *Migration Theory-Talking Across Disciplines*, London, New York: Routledge.

House of Commons, 1958, "The Tablet," December 5, p. 1563.

Hughes, Carleste, 2001, "Lives On Hold-American Greets Some Refugees From Oppressive Nations With Strict Incarceration in a Brick Building in Jamaica," *Newsday*, June 3, p. G6.

Huntington, Samuel P., 1993, "The Clash of Civilizations," *Foreign Affairs*, Summer, 22–49.

Huntington, Samuel P., 1996, "The West: Unique, Not Universal," *Foreign Affairs*, 75(6), 28–46.

Huntington, Samuel P., 2000, "Reconsidering Immigration – Is Mexico a Special Case," *Backgrounder*, November, http://www.cis.org/articles/2000/back1100.html.

Huntington, Samuel P., 2000, "The Special Case of Mexican Immigration – Why Mexico Is a Problem," *American Enterprise*, online edition, December, http://www.theamericanenterprise.org/taedec00c.html.

Huntington, Samuel P., 2001, "Migration Flows Are the Central Issue of Our Time," *International Herald Tribune*, February 2, Internet edition.

INS, 2000, "Border Safety Initiative," http://www.ins.usdoj.gov.

INS, 2000, "National Border Patrol Strategy," *Immigration and Naturalization Service*, http://www.ins.usdoj.gov.

INS, 2001, "U.S. and Mexico Announce Expanded Efforts to Save Migrant Lives – Binational Strategy Includes Intensified Focus on High Risk Areas," June 15.

Institute of Race Relations, 2001, "The Dispersal of Xenophobia," February 15, online edition.

Jackson, Thomas, 1995, "Immigration: The Debate Becomes Interesting," *American Renaissance*, 6(7), http://www.amren.com, Internet edition.

Jacobson, David, 1997, *Rights Across Borders – Immigration and the Decline of Citizenship*, Baltimore: Johns Hopkins University Press.

Johnson, Kevin, 2001, "Va. Group Accused of Illegal Efforts for Racist U.K. Party," *USA Today*, September 2, p. 4A.

Kamber, Michael, 2001, "A Link in the Chain," *Village Voice*, April 11–17, online edition.

Kamber, Michael, 2001, "Deadly Game – Crossing to the Other Side," *Village Voice*, April 18–24, online edition.

Kanstroom, Daniel, 1996, "Dangerous Undertones of the New Nativism," Juan F. Perea (ed.), *Immigrants Out! – The New Nativism and the Anti-Immigrant Impulse in the United States*, New York and London: New York University Press.

Kearney, Michael, 1991, "Borders and Boundaries of State at the End of Empire," *Journal of Historical Sociology*, 4(1), 53–71.

Kennedy, Paul, 1993, *Preparing for the Twenty-First Century*, New York: Random House.

Kim, Lucian, 2001, "Britain Wants a Wider Mote Around 'Fortress Europe'," *Christian Science Monitor*, February 22.

Kofman, Eleonore and Gillian Youngs (eds), 1999, *Globalization – Theory and Practice*, London: Pinter.

Kristeva, Julia, 1991, *Stranger to Ourselves*, New York: Columbia University Press.

Kushnick, Louis, 1998, *Race, Class and Struggle – Essays on Racism and Inequality in Britain, the U.S., and Western Europe*, London: Rivers Oram Press.

Lattimer, Mark, 1999, "When Labour Played the Racist Card," *New Statesman*, January 22, Internet edition.

Layton-Henry, Zig, 1984, *The Politics of Race in Britain*, London: Allen and Unwin.

Le Quesne, Nicholas, 2001, "Just Within Reach," *Time-Europe*, September 2, Internet edition.

Llorente, Elizabeth, 2001, "Asylum Comes with Bars," *The Bergen Record*, January 28.

Lloyd, Cathie and Hazel Waters, 1991, "France: One Culture, One People?" *Race and Class*, 32(3), 49–65.

Lloyd-Roberts, Sue, 2001, "Britain's Jailed Asylum Seekers," *BBC News*, August 23, Internet edition.

Los Angeles Times, 2000, "Churches Target Border-Crossing Deaths," December 27, Internet edition.

MacMaster, Neil, 1991, "The 'Seuill de Tolerance': The Uses of a 'Scientific' Racist Concept," in *Race, Discourse, and Power in France*, Maxim Silverman (ed.), Aldershot: Gower.

Malone, Dan, 2001, "Asylum Awaits Liberian Detained Six Years," *Washington Post*, January 21, Internet edition.

Manzo, Kathryn A., 1996, *Creating Boundaries – The Politics of Race and Nation*, Colorado: Lynne Rienner.

Marcus, Jonathon, 1995, *The National Front and French Politics*, Basingstoke: Macmillan.

Marcuse, Herbert, 1964, *One-Dimensional Man*, Boston: Beacon Press.

Margaronis, Maria, 2001, "Europe's Unwelcome Guests," *The Nation*, May 27, pp. 14–20.

Martin, Gary, 1999, "INS Deports Record Number of Undocumented Immigrants," *San Antonio Express*, January 8, online edition.

Martin, Philipe and Jonas Widgren, "International Migration: Facing the Challenge," *Population Reference Bureau*, March 2002.

Massumi, Brian, 1996, *A User's Guide to Capitalism and Schizophrenia – Deviations from Deleuze and Guattari*, Cambridge and London: MIT Press.

Meissner, Doris, Robert Hormats, Antonio Walker, and Shijuro Ogata, 1993, *International Migration Challenges in a New Era. A Report to the Trilateral Commission*, New York, Paris, and Tokyo: The Trilateral Commission.

Messina, Anthony M. *et al.* (eds), 1992, *Ethnic and Racial Minorities in Advanced Industrial Democracies*, Westport: Greenwood Press, Inc.

Migration News, 1996, "French Police Remove Immigrants from Church," 3(9).

Migration News, 1996, "France Amends 1993 Immigration Law," 3(12).

Migration News, 1997, "France: Immigration Reform Approved," 4(3).

Migration News, 1997, "Current Information Issues," 4(4).
Migration News, 1997, "France Amends Immigration Law," 4(4).
Migration News, 1997, "Immigrants and Welfare," 4(6).
Migration News, 1997, "France: Repeal Immigration Laws," 4(7).
Migration News, 1997, "French Immigration Bill," 4(12).
Migration News, 1998, "France: Law, National Front," 5(4).
Migration News, 1998, "France: 70,000 Get Amnesty," 5(7).
Migration News, 1998, "France: Vatican, Politics," 5(9).
Migration News, 1998, "INS. Sanctions, Detention Fees," October.
Migration News, 1999, "France: National Front," 6(1).
Migration News, 1999, "France: National Front, Headscarves," 6(2).
Migration News, 2002, "France: Le Pen," May.
Migration News, 2000, 7(11).
Miles, Jack, 1995, "The Coming Immigration Debate," *The Atlantic Monthly*, April.
Miles, Robert, 1993, *Racism After "Race Relation,"* London: Routledge.
Miles, Robert and Annie Phizacklea, 1984, *White Man's Country – Racism in British Politics*, London: Pluto Press.
Miller, Greg, and Patrick J. McDonnell, 2001, "Immigration Task Force to Urge Policy Overhaul," *The Los Angeles Times*, July 15, wire service.
Mitchell, Christopher, 1989, "International Migration, International Relations and Foreign Policy," *International Migration Review*, 23(3), 681–708.
Money, Jeannette, 1999, *Fences and Neighbors – The Political Geography of Immigration Control*, Ithaca and London: Cornell University Press.
Nair, Sami, 1996, "France: A Crisis of Integration," *Dissent*, 43(3).
National Intelligence Council, 2000, "National Intelligence Estimate: The Global Infectious Disease Threat and Its Implications for the U.S.," Environment Report, Change and Security Project, The Woodrow Wilson Center, Summer, 33–65.
Nermin, Abadan-Unat, 1987, "Summary of the Main Results of Conference of OECD Working Party," *The Future of Migration*, Paris: OECD.
Nevins, Joseph, 2002, Operation Gate Keeper. The Rise of the "Illegal Alien" and the Making of the U.S. – Mexico Boundary, New York and London: Routledge.
New York Times, 2001, "Australian Troops Board Refugee Ship," August 29, Internet edition.
Norris, Christopher, 1992, *Uncritical Theory – Postmodernism, Intellectuals and the Gulf War*, Boston: University of Massachusetts Press.
O'Connell, Christian E., 1996, "Plight of France's *Sans-Papiers* Gives a Face to Struggle Over Immigration," *The Human Rights Brief*.
Ojita, Mirta, 1998, "Change in Laws Sets Off Big Wave of Deportation," *New York Times*, December 15.
Oliver, Mark, 2002, "Drowning Street Denies 'Dumping' Refugees," *Guardian Unlimited*, May 14.
Osborne, Cyril, 1961, *House of Commons*, August, 1320–1321.
Panitch, Leo, 1996, "Rethinking the Role of the State," in *Globalization – Critical Reflections*, James Mittelman (ed.), Boulder: Lynne Reinner.

Polanyi, Karl, 1994, *The Great Transformation*, Boston: Beacon Press,
Procacci, Giovanna, 1991, "Social Economy and the Government of Poverty," in *The Foucault Effect – Studies in Governmentality*, Graham Burchell, Colin Gordon, and Peter Miller (eds), Chicago: University of Chicago Press.
Reese, Tom, 1982, "Immigration Policies in the United Kingdom," in *Race in Britain – Continuity and Change*, Charles Husband (ed.), London: Hutchinson.
Reimers, David M., 1992, *Still the Golden Door – The Third World Comes to America*, New York: Columbia University Press.
Richburg, Keith B., 2001, "At Spain's Gate, Africans Dream of Europe," *Washington Post*, March 28, p. A01.
Richmond, Anthony H., 1994, *Global Apartheid – Refugees, Racism, and the New World Order*, Oxford: Oxford University Press.
Rosenau, James, 1997, *Along the Domestic–Foreign Frontier: Exploring Governance in a Turbulent World*, London: Cambridge University Press.
Runnymead, Trust, 2000, *The Report of the Commission on the Future of Multi-Ethnic Britain*.
Sach, Susan, 2001, "Second Thought: Cracking the Door for Immigrants," *The New York Times*, July 1, online edition.
Salopek, Paul, 2001, "Intolerance in 'Rainbow Nation'," *The Chicago Tribune*, January 16, Internet edition.
Scarp, Mark J. and Krist Baxter, 1999, "Chandler Settles Roundup Lawsuit," *East Valley Tribune*, February 11, pp. A1 and A14.
Schlesinger, Arthur M. Jr, 1992, *The Disuniting of America – Reflections on a Multicultural Society*, W.W. Norton and Company, p. 17.
Schmitt, Eric, 2001, "Bush Aides Weigh Legalizing Status of Mexicans is U.S.," *The New York Times*, July 15, Internet edition.
Schuck, Peter H., 1996, "Alien Rumination: What Immigrant Have Wrought in America," *Yale Law Journal*, 105(5), 1963–2012.
Shehnaz, Suterwalla, Barbie Nadeau, Emma Daly, Rita O'Reilly, Christian Caryl, and Stefan Theil, 2001, "Immigration and Reality – Europe has a Choice: Abandon Zero Immigration or Let Its Labor Market Suffer," *Newsweek*, January 28, web exclusive, http://www.msnbc.com/news/522494.asp?cp1 = 1.
Silverman, Max, 1992, *Deconstructing the Nation: Immigration, Racism, and Citizenship in Modern France*, London: Routledge.
Silverman, Max, 1999, *Facing Postmodernity. Contemporary French Thought on Culture and Society*, London: Routledge.
Simmel, Georg, 1908, "The Stranger," in *On Individuality and Social Forms*, Donald N. Levine (ed.), Chicago: University of Chicago Press.
Simons, Marlise, 2000, "At Home Resentment Hits Immigrants," *International Herald Tribune*, February 15, Internet edition.
Singer, Rena, 2000, "South Africa's Brutal New Bias," *The Christian Science Monitor*, August 31, Internet edition.
Sivanandan, A., 2001, "The Emergence of Xeno-Racism," *Institute of Race Relations*, July.

Skerry, Peter, 1996, "Missing the Boast-Immigration Law Demonizes Foreigners But Solves Little," *Washington Post,* October 20.

Smith, R. Jeffery, 2000, "Europe Bids Immigrants Unwelcome," *The Washington Post Foreign Service,* July 23, p. A01.

Socolovsky, Jerome, 2001, "Nine Miles to a Better Life," *Chicago Sun Times,* August 19, Internet edition.

Solomon, John, 1993, *Race and Racism in Britain,* London: The MacMillan Press.

SOPEMI, 1992, *Continuous Reporting System on Migration. Trends in International Migration,* Paris: Organization For Economic Cooperation and Development.

Southern Poverty Law Center's Intelligence Reports, 2001, "Blood on the Border," Spring, No. 101.

Southern Poverty Law Center's Intelligence Reports, 2001, "Hand Across the Water," Fall, No. 103.

Soysal, Yasemin, 1994, *Limits of Citizenship: Migrant and Postnational Membership in Europe,* Chicago: University of Chicago Press.

Stalker, Peter, 2000, *Workers Without Frontiers – The Impact of Globalization on International Migration,* Colorado: Lynne Rienner Publishers.

Stanley, Bruce, 2001, "Illegal Immigrants Plagues Chunnel," *Washington Post,* August 24, Internet edition.

Steele, Jonathon, 2000, "Fortress Europe Confronts the Unthinkable," *Guardian Unlimited,* October 30.

Taguieff, Pierre-Andre, 1990, "The New Cultural Racism in France," *Telos,* No. 83, 109–122.

Taylor, Jeffery, 2000, "Another French Revolution – In Marseilles, Europe Confronts Its North African Future," *Harpers Magazine,* November, 58–66.

Teitelbaum, Michael S. 1984, "Immigration, Refugees, and Foreign Policy," *International Organization,* 38(3), 429–448.

Tobar, Hector, 1998, "An Ugly Stain On City's Bright and Shining Plan, Raid: In A Roundup of Illegal Immigrants, Chandler, Arizona Snared Many U.S. Citizens Who 'Looked' Mexican," *Los Angeles Times,* December 28, Internet edition.

Travis, Alan, 2000, "British Tag is Coded Racism," *Guardian,* October 11.

Travis, Alan, 2002, "Minister Stirs Row Over Plans for 15 New Centres," *Guardian Unlimited,* May 15.

Trueheart, Charles, 2000, "Fear of the 'Other' Fuels Rise of European Rightists," *International Herald Tribune,* February 12, Internet edition.

Trueheart, Charles, 2000, "Racism Persists Despite Egalitarian Creed," *Washington Post,* June 11, p. A25.

Vaillant, Emmanuel, 1997, "Making Them Legal," *Le Monde Diplomatique,* November, Internet edition.

Vasagar, Jeevan, 2000, "Three Sought for Racist Attack on Turk," *The Guardian Unlimited,* December 28, Internet edition.

Vaughan-Morgan, J., 1965, *House of Commons*, March 23, p. 359.

Viviano, Frank, 1999, "Europe Suddenly Doesn't Even Recognize Itself," *San Francisco Chronicle*, March 5, p. A1.

Waldman, Amy, 1999, "The Diallo Shooting: The Overview; 4 Officer Enter Not-Guilty please to Murder Counts in Diallo Case," *New York Times*, April 1, Internet archives.

Walker, David, 2001, "Welcome to Britain," *Guardian*, January 29, Internet edition.

Walzer, Michael, 1983, *Spheres of Justice*, New York: Basic Books.

Walvin, James, 1984, *Passage to Britain – Immigration in British History and Politics*, Middlesex, England: Penguin Books.

Webber, Frances, 1991, "From Ethnocentrism to Euro-Racism," *Race and Class*, 32(3), 11–17.

Weiner, Myron, 1992/93, "Security, Stability, and International Migration," *International Security*, 17(3), 91–126.

Weiner, Myron, 1995, *The Global Migration Crisis: Challenge to States and to Human Rights*, New York: Harper Collins.

Western, John, 1992, *A Passage to England*, Minneapolis: University of Minnesota Press.

Winant, Howard, 1994, *Racial Conditions*, Minneapolis: University of Minnesota Press.

Wierviorka, Michel, 1995, *The Arena of Racism*, London: Sage Publications.

Wolfe, Alan, 1978, *The Seamy Side of Democracy – Repression in America*, New York and London: Longman.

World Migration Report 2000, International Organization for Migration, November.

Young, Robert J.C., 1995, *Colonial Desire – Hybridity in Theory, Culture, and Race*, London and New York: Routledge.

Younge, Gary, 2001, "The West Wants the Free Movement of Capital, But Not of Labour. It Is Illogical and Immoral," *Guardian Unlimited*, March 19, Internet edition.

Zoellner, Tom, 2001, "Mexico Says Legalize Crossers or No Deal," *The Arizona Republic*, June 22.

Index

AFL–CIO 42
ambivalence 6
anarchy 9
Andreas, Peter 5, 6, 29, 78, 85
anti-immigrantism 1, 4, 15, 22–3, 70
anxiety 58, 73
Anzaldua, Gloria 89
Ashley, Richard 79
assimilation 58, 65
asylum 35, 40, 54, 57
Asylum and Immigration Bill 1999 55

Bader, Veit 83
Balibar, Etienne 19, 24, 66, 98
Barker, Martin 19, 82
Barre, Raymond 64
Bauman, Zygmunt 6, 29, 71, 79, 84–5
Bevan, Vaughan 91
Bhabha, Homi 16, 27, 62, 84
Bonnet, Christian 64–5
border 2, 25–6; control 33; deaths 33, 86; US/Mexican 13
Border Patrol 34, 38
BORSTAR 86
boundaries 24
Bracero Program 34, 38
Brah, Avtar 21, 51, 83, 91
Brimlow, Peter 4, 22, 24, 38, 78, 83
Britain 16–17, 19, 44
British Nationality Act 45
British National Party 93

Calavita, Kitty 32, 79, 85
Callaghan, James 48
Calvez, M. Corentin 63
Campaign Against Racism and Fascism 56
Campbell, David 81
capitalism 11–12, 15, 77
Castaneda, Jorge 85
Castoriada, Cornelius 98
Channel Tunnel 44, 71
Chevenement, Jean-Pierre 69
citizenship stripping 38
codes 10–11, 26; social 39
coding 18
Cohen, Roger 78
commodity fiction 6, 8
Commonwealth 45, 47
Commonwealth Immigrants Act 1962 45, 48
Connolly, William 10, 79
Constable, Marianne 41, 89
Cornelius Wayne 78, 88
criminality 51
cultural fence 29
culture 24

danger 40; social 61
dangerous class 27, 51
Debre, Jean-Louis 68–9
Debre Law 66, 68
decoded flows 11
decoding 11
Deleuze, Gilles 3, 9–10, 16, 28, 39–40, 43
democracies 16

democratic 13
Der Derian, James 81
Derrida, Jacques 11, 16–17
desire 1–3, 6, 10, 12; for order 13,
    27, 33, 39, 47–8, 57; social
    theory of 9
desiring production 10
despotic machine 11, 13
deterritorialization 11–12, 60
Diallo, Amadou 13
difference 18, 21; cultural 24, 50,
    64; racial 45
differentiation 40
disorder 9, 45
dispersal 30, 47, 49
distancing 29
Doty, Roxanne 79, 84–5, 92
Dover 55
Dunn, Timothy 41, 88

Enloe, Cynthia 25, 84
European Union 3, 4
exclusion 10, 14, 18, 28
exteriorization 37

fascism 10, 13
FBI 34
Fix, Michael 38, 86–7
flows 3, 28, 33, 62
Foucault, Michel 6, 9, 15, 37
France 3–4, 16–17, 25
Frankel, Joseph 90
Freeman, Gary 94

GAO 41
Gardner, Joy 13
Gilroy, Paul 84
globalization 2–6, 9, 17, 32; thesis 5
Goldberg, David Theo 21
Gordon, Colin 84
governmentality 6, 8–9, 60
Grovogui, Siba 81
Guattari, Felix 3, 9–10, 16, 28,
    39–40, 43

Hargreaves, Alec G. 95
Hattersly, Ray 50, 57, 94
Hernu, Charles 63
Hobsbawm, Eric 23, 83

Hollifield, James 78
Hornsby Smith, Patricia 52
human nature 19–20
Huntington, Samuel 23–4, 78, 83

identity 1, 9, 21, 74; cultural 24;
    French 60; national 24
Illegal Immigration Reform and
    Immigrant Responsibility Act
    1996 33–4, 39, 42
immigration 2–4, 6, 16; illegal 5,
    33, 39–41; and racism 18
Immigration Act of 1971 49–50, 52
Immigration and Financial
    Responsibility Act 1996 32
Immigration and Naturalization
    Service 34, 36, 38, 42
Imperial Beach 34
inclusion 10, 14
inside 6
Institute of Race Relations 93
international relations 17

Jacobson, David 78, 91
Jamaica 45
Jeanneney, Jean-Marcel 59
judicial review 35
jus soil 50

Kearney, Michael 32, 43, 85
Kennedy, Paul 5, 78
Kristeva, Julia 26

labor 32–3, 39, 59–60
laissez faire 58–9
Le Pen, Jean Marie 66, 70, 97
liberalism 8
Lloyd, Cathie 96

Manzo, Kathryn 21, 83, 91
Marcuse, Herbert 79
Martin, Phillip 78
Massenet, Michel 63
meatpacking 42
methods 15, 17
Mexico 3, 16
migration 2
Miles, Robert 78, 82
Mitterand, François 64

Nair, Sami 96
nation 17, 19, 51
National Front (FN) 66
National Immigration Office
(ONI) 59
neo-racism 15, 19–22, 24, 45
neo-territorialities 40
new racism 15, 19, 20, 62
nomads 14; nomadism 39
Notting Hill 53

OECD 3
Operation Gatekeeper 13, 15,
34, 79
Operation Hold the Line 34, 85
Operation Last Call 39
Operation Restoration 38
Operation Safeguard 34
order 1, 5–6, 13, 17
Osborne, Cyril 46
outside 6
overcoding 13

Pasqua, Charles 66
Pasqua Law 66–7
pauper 14, 25–7, 31
pedagogical 28, 62
Personal Responsibility and Work
Opportunity Reconciliation Act
of 1996 33–4, 36
Polanyi, Karl 6, 9, 37, 79
poles: of desire 10–11, 33;
schizophrenic 5, 9–10, 33,
58–9
political space 14
population: floating 40
Population Reference Bureau 90
Postal-Vinay, Antoine 61, 95
Powell, Enoch 47, 49
Proposition 187 15

race 21, 24, 51
racial threshold 48
racism 14–19, 21, 23; cultural 21;
differentialist 19
Red Cross 44, 71
reterritorialization 9, 11–12, 33
Richmond, Anthony H. 22, 30
rights 5, 33, 40

Rosenau, James 5
Runnymede Trust 94

San Diego 34
Sangatte 71
Sans Papiers 67–9
Schlesinger, Arthur M. 4, 78
security 1, 6
seuil de tolerance 58, 62–3, 65,
94, 96
Shapiro, Michael 81
Silverman, Max 21, 25, 30
Simmel, Georg 26
Simpson, Alan 34
Sivanandan, A. 93
social order 26, 45
social production 10
social protection 8–9
social welfare 62
socius 11
Soguk, Nevzat 79
Solomon, John 91
SOPEMI 78
Southern Poverty Law Center 73
sovereignty 2, 4–5, 8, 17
space 2–3, 25
speed 3
state 10–12, 26; violence 14
statecraft 1–2, 9, 12, 17, 25, 27–8
stereotype 6
Stoleru, Lionel 64
stranger 25–6, 66
Straw, Jack 56

Taguieff, Pierre-Andre 21
territorial 3, 28; boundaries 2
territorialization 9, 18
terrorism 2
Thatcher, Margaret 4
Third World 2, 4, 6, 16, 19, 32, 45;
immigrants 25
threshold of tolerance 46

UDA 33
United Kingdom 4
United States 3, 16–17, 21
Urban Institute 37
Urstaat 11, 13, 33; *see also* despotic
machine

violence 13, 19; racial 19;
    structural 13

Walvin, James 91
Walzer, Michael 24, 83
Western, John 90
whiteness 57
Wievorka, Michel 21

Wilson, Harold 48
Winant, Howard 20, 82–3
Wolfe, Alan 79

xenophobia 19, 30

Zimmerman, Wendy 38, 86–7